Chaos
to
Clarity

Other Books by Rev. Patricia Cagganello

God is in the Little Things: Messages from the Animals
God is in the Little Things: Messages from the Golden Angels
Scanning for Signal (Co-Author)

Other Books by Kathleen O'Keefe-Kanavos

Surviving Cancerland: Intuitive Aspects of Healing
Dreams That Can Save Your Life: Early Warning Signs of Cancer and Other Diseases (Co-Author)

Sacred Stories of Transformational Change

Chaos
to
Clarity

Rev. Patricia Cagganello &
Kathleen O'Keefe-Kanavos

Sacred Stories
PUBLISHING

Chaos to Clarity: Sacred Stories of Transformational Change
Rev. Patricia Cagganello and Kathleen O'Keefe-Kanavos

Tradepaper ISBN: 978-1-945026-61-4
Electronic ISBN: 978-1-945026-62-1

Library of Congress Control Number: 2019951248

Published by Sacred Stories Publishing, Fort Lauderdale, FL USA

*These are the Sacred Stories of our time.
Powerful voices from around the globe that
speak to our shared human experience.
May they inspire you and give you great hope.*

TABLE OF CONTENTS

ACKNOWLEDGMENTS

This book has been a collaborative work on many levels. Thank you Patricia Cagganello of Sacred Stories Publishing for your invitation to write this first book of our anthology series together. It has been a joy being your partner in this literary pursuit. A big thanks to Dennis Pitocco, of BIZCATALYST 360° for his support for this endeavor. The dedication and generous sharing of deeply personal information by authors gave the book a depth of sympathy and empathy necessary for clarity and healing in the face of life's chaotic storms.

And, without the emotional support and understanding of my husband, Peter Kanavos, this book's deadlines may not have been met. Many a night he made dinner for us both, fed the cats, and canceled couple-plans and trips so I could, continue to work in the "Kat-Rat-Hole," the name he affectionately gave my office. Honey, I love you!

-Kathleen O'Keefe-Kanavos

Thank you to the courageous individuals, *aka our contributing authors,* for having the selflessness to share their life changing, personal stories with us. It takes a special kind of warrior to bare their soul for the world to see; to give others hope and inspiration. Thank you to our readers for showing up and having the courage to read these stories. You have a depth to your soul that must be acknowledged. Please know that you are not alone in your experiences. May we all hold each other's hearts with gentleness and love.

And finally, thank you to my co-author Kat Kanavos for making me laugh and reminding me to enjoy the long and winding road of our co-creative process and this crazy little thing called life!

-Rev. Patricia Cagganello

FOREWORD

Loss, Gain, and Change
by Bernie Siegel, MD

To everything there is a season; And a time to every
purpose under the sun; A time to get and a time to lose;
A time to keep and a time to cast away;

~ Ecclesiastes 3:1-8

What the caterpillar calls the end of the world,
the Master calls a butterfly.[1]

~ Richard Bach

The earthworm is my role model and mentor for handling change. It can swallow anything you throw at it, turn it into rich fertilizer, and make it a positive growth experience. In much the same way, coal under great pressure becomes a diamond.

My feelings about change and loss can be very different.

Loss and change can relate to objects and material things that do not experience feelings such as pain, love, or consciousness. So, I can lose my health, or my car keys, or even my house if it burns down—but when one of our pets dies, or one of our children leaves home, we don't lose them. Their consciousness remains with us, although our life has now changed due to their physical absence, and you can't physically replace what is dead. Now you have to learn the role change plays in your life.

Change is a labor pain through which we can give birth to a new self and life, which makes the pain meaningful and justified.

The most significant preparation for life and the changes we must all confront is growing up with parents who love you. Ninety-eight percent of Harvard University students who said that they did not have loving parents suffered a significant illness by middle age, while only 24 percent of those who felt loved did.

I was born to a very sick mother who was told by her physicians not to become pregnant because it might threaten her life. She became pregnant anyhow because her mother wanted a grandchild. When they finally pulled me out of my mother, had it not been for a loving grandmother who spent many months "pushing things back where they belonged" who knows where I'd be today? Touch makes a difference.

Because of the difficult childhoods my parents experienced, I received mottoes to live by as I grew up. My dad's father died of tuberculosis, leaving six children and his wife with nothing. My mom's family had to escape from Russia to survive.

Here are their mottoes, which I did not appreciate as a child. I sought solutions, not advice.

1. "Mom, I have a problem, and I don't know what to do."
   "Do what makes you happy."
2. "Mom, I had a terrible day. Everything went wrong."
   "God is redirecting you. Something good will come of this."

My father said that his father dying when he was twelve was one of the best things that ever happened to him. I couldn't understand what he was talking about until he said, "It taught me what was important about life."

I learned early on that sometimes a curse can become a blessing. He was always helping people to survive and thrive, and that memory gets me through tough times and helps me deal with people who abuse me.

I have learned to be a love warrior.

Yes, love is my weapon, and it blows violent people away. I don't have space to tell you all that goes into this, but try saying "I love you!" to people who are a problem and watch their reaction.

Norman Vincent Peale said his mom used to say, "Norman, if God closes one door, further down the corridor, another will be open." When you grow up with hope in your heart, you know there will be another door. You can handle change and the labor pains of life by giving birth to yourself.

As the Bible tells us, help your neighbor find what they have lost. Be it their health or car keys. God never punishes you by taking things from you. God is a healing resource through faith. I have had patients who went home to die and returned free of cancer. When asked how she did it, one woman said, "I left my troubles to God."

I had a near-death experience as a four-year-old.

I can tell you from experience that our consciousness doesn't die when our body is lost. I have learned that we are not our bodies. Our bodies are the tools we are given so that we can make a difference. We are spirit, soul, and consciousness. These things learn but do not change, as your body and emotions can and do. I think past-life experiences are also part of this experience of the eternal life of our consciousness, which is never lost but becomes recycled through those who come after us. When you see a five-year-old on TV playing the violin at the level of a master, that is the result of past-life experiences.

Death is the ultimate change experienced by everyone.

In the hospital, death is seen as a failure and a lost battle. Rarely do you hear the word "dead" used when a patient dies. People say the deceased are lost, passed, gone. At Yale, when my friend Alan died, I was told he had "Brady'd." The morgue is in the Brady building, so people didn't say he died—he Brady'd.

Most people choose to lose their lives at night in the hospital, so the doctor won't be there to interfere with their dying. One doctor wrote an article entitled, *Not on My Shift* when he realized that he and two other doctors, all on eight-hour shifts, were keeping a man from dying in the ICU. He let the man die when he realized how cruel and senseless their actions were. Life is an experience, and although disease or tragedy may cause us to lose our life, it is essential that we love our lives and bodies. If we fight a battle against illness, we empower the enemy instead of healing our lives and bodies.

When we die, we become perfect again. Many cases verify that. People born blind could see during near-death experiences. When we die, we become dreamless, unalive, and perfect again.

I think of death as a *commencement*. Why is it that a graduation is called a commencement and not a termination? Hey, you are finished with school. Why do we describe it as just beginning? Because that is the nature of life.

Loss is change, and change is a commencement.

One thing I would ask you to lose forever is the fear of loss. When you live in fear of loss, you do not live. I ask you to lose your fear of living and the difficulties you create in your mind. Fear is a helpful feeling when a vicious animal threatens you. Then you run and climb and do things a calm person could not achieve because you are motivated and empowered by the fear. But when you fear what is not reality but just your mind's problems, you are more likely to lose your life. The constant, unreal fear of loss can have adverse effects on your health.

If you have love, you will never be at a loss or be unable to survive loss because you are complete. I know from our love, how my wife and I were complete when we were together. We did not need anyone or anything. We had it all because we had each other and our love for each other. No change, event, or disease could separate us.

It is also essential to love yourself, no matter how much parents and others abused you—even if they asked you to commit suicide. I know children who have experienced this. But when I became their CD, or Chosen Dad, and helped them to see themselves as children of God, they did not lose their lives—they created them. When you know, accept, and see your beauty and divinity, you can't lose yourself, no matter what others do or say. You find yourself as you never had before. When you become a CD or CM (Chosen Mother), you can rebirth people and help them become children of God.

Change does not have to be interpreted as loss.

We all experience change; it is the nature of life. Change can be seen as a labor pain of life that leads to a rebirth rather than a loss of the life you desired. Meaning can never be lost from your life unless you encounter circumstances that eliminate it from your mind and make you feel your life has lost all meaning. Dr. Viktor Frankl, an Austrian neurologist and psychiatrist, known for his Existential Therapy, learned this in a concentration camp and shared it in his book, *Man's Search for Meaning*: "To live is to suffer. To survive is to find meaning in the suffering."[2] But, first, you have to stop focusing on the suffering and find ways to give your life meaning, before you lose your life. When you change someone's life in a meaningful way, you become real and immortal through love.

"Love is immortal, while hate dies every minute."

When you fill your mind with hate, you do not see the truth. Think about being rejected and pushed out of your nest, as the Ugly Duckling was in Hans Christian Andersen's tale. The duckling didn't go off and spend his life hating his mother and seeking revenge. Or consider the tiger whose mother died after giving birth in a parable often told by mythology author Joseph Campbell. The tiger was raised by the goats his mother had been chasing, so he thought he was a goat. How did these creatures, who had lost their identity, allow themselves to find peace and truth and healing?

I found the answer to the world's problems is a quiet mind.

Let me compare a turbulent mind to water that is being blown by strong winds or a whirlpool. You cannot see your reflection in the turbulence, but what happens when the wind dies down, and the water is still? The truth is revealed to the quiet mind, which can then communicate with all of creation and consciousness. The quiet mind and still pond reflect the truth—but you have to create that stillness and lose all the disturbing emotions. Otherwise, the ugly duckling would have never been able to see he was a swan. The tiger also was taken to a still pond by another tiger, who told him to look and see he was a tiger and not a goat. The quiet mind is like a state of meditation, and the truth you find can heal you and your life. What you lose are your wounds and the untruths you were exposed to. Then you can release the life imposed on you and find your true beauty.

Loss is not failure; not living is failure. So, lose your untrue self and become your true and authentic self. Find what you lost. Do not wait for a disaster or life-threatening illness to wake you up so you can start your search for your true self. In one study, 95 percent of lottery winners said winning was the worst thing that ever happened to them. Why? Because they didn't learn what my father had learned as a child—what was important about life. I hope to win someday so I can help improve the world and become family for many people.

Let me close with some thoughts that have helped me.

One is that what we call loss can be defined as change and that change can bring something new into your life. Labor pain leads to the birth of a new life. In the same way, loss can be the pain that stimulates and produces new growth in your life.

Once you open your mind to this concept, you will turn every curse into a blessing. Although everything is impermanent, a loss can become a gain if you maintain a quiet mind and allow yourself to see the truth. As psychologist Carl Jung said, "The future is unconsciously prepared long in advance and, therefore, can be guessed by clairvoyants." And I know that is true from my work with patients' dreams and drawings. There are no coincidences.

Perfection is not creation. It is a magic trick, and loss can be God's redirection. When you realize that, you will see how the loss of life is not about losing but about choosing a new life and rebirthing your soul and spirit. You will embrace loss like a graduation and not a termination. Imagine getting a flat tire on the way to the airport, only to learn you missed a flight that had crashed after take-off. That apparent loss saved your life.

I will conclude with the death or loss-of-life-experience we had when the lives of my father, father-in-law, and a patient occurred. A hospice lawyer refused to allow the removal of a feeding tube from a dying, comatose woman, despite her family's desires. The lawyer said, "You are murdering her." Because we can hear in a coma, I stood by her bedside and told her that her family was beside her and if she needed to go, it was alright, because her love would stay with them. She died peacefully a few minutes later with no conflict.

My quadriplegic father-in-law, at age ninety-seven, told us, "No dinner. No pills tonight." He died quietly in his sleep that evening, as did my wife years later on the same date her father had died.

My dad told my mother, "I need to get out of here." I told Mom he was talking about his body and not his bed. So, he had a day set aside for him to die, and we let our family know so they could come and be with him. The day he chose to die, a voice told me, "Ask your mother how your folks met." So, I did when I arrived at the hospital.

My mother said that my father had lost a coin toss and had to take her out on a date. She went on with more stories, which had everyone laughing. My father died laughing. He looked so well that I thought he was going to change his mind. But when the last family member arrived, he took his last breath and became perfect again, although he had no way of consciously knowing who was coming last.

Dad didn't lose his life. He gave us all more and better lives.

Remember, when you are confronting a loss and change in your life, you can always ask for help. That is a survival strategy. We are here to restore, heal, and guide each other. So, share your loss and wounds with those who are natives; those who have loved and healed what you are experiencing and have survived and thrived. They can be your life coaches and help you survive change and loss.

True faith can overcome every change and loss.

My wife died eighteen months before I wrote these words. We were married for sixty-three years. What has changed is that I have lost her physical body, and it makes my life feel emptier than it ever has been. But at the same time, I still have her with me. What do I mean by that? I mean that her humor, beauty, love, and spirit are always beside me and will never be lost. As many wise authors note, love is immortal, and it makes all things immortal. The bridge between the land of the living and the land of the dead is love.

I know my wife is perfect again, and I am grateful to have had messages from her spirit and consciousness since she died through a mystic who was a patient of mine. Some messages she brings me directly, and other signs I detect—like pennies from Heaven and the number nine (her birthday was 9/9) appearing on my medical wrist band. Those are without question signs from my beloved wife.

So, I leave you with this poem, written by me, knowing my beloved wife Bobbie is alright and wants me to feel her support. As my mother shared, "God is redirecting you. Something good will come of this."

The Great Teacher

Death, what a great teacher you are
Yet few of us elect to take your class
And learn about life
That is the essence of death's teaching
Death is not an elective
We must all take the class
The wise students audit the class in their early years
And find enlightenment
They are prepared when graduation day comes
It is your commencement

The Spirituality of Change
by Rev. Patricia Cagganello

In the experience is the emotion, and in the emotion is the gift.

The spiritual journey is one of change. It is an opportunity to expand our awareness of the consciousness we hold, and to transform our limited and limiting beliefs to encompass the wholeness of who we are and our part in our larger Collective journey.

Every story is a sacred story.

There is a power and a resonance in our stories, our shared experiences. I have learned that *in the experience of our story is the emotion and in the emotion is our gift.* In the gift of emotion is where we can find compassion for ourselves and expand our awareness of the whole.

Important events in our lives are our opportunities to do this; they are our change agents. The more significant the event—or rather, the more significant the emotion the event generates—the more attention we pay, and the greater the opportunity we have for transformation.

Many people today hold to the belief that these events must be traumatic. In some cases, they are. In this book, you will read stories of profound grief and loss. The courageous individuals who wrote them are to be applauded for their willingness to be of service to others. They share their most painful stories so others may know they are not alone, and there truly is light waiting at the end of the tunnel. These are examples of individuals who have gone through a spiritual transformation and are now holding a consciousness of selflessness.

However, the good news is, the experience of spiritual transformation is not a punitive life sentence we must serve. Rather, it can be a joyful experience we choose to have. This book also includes narratives of great change experienced through love, joy, and beautiful life-changing events.

All these stories have something in common: The individuals experiencing the change developed a new and expanded perception of themselves and of the lives they are choosing to live. They have moved through chaos to clarity. As I said, not every story has a happy ending, but they all have an ending where the men and women emerged with a deep appreciation for the wisdom they have gained.

In my personal life, I have experienced significant change.

I was the quintessential fifty-year-old, middle-aged, suburban, U.S. soccer mom leading a relatively happy, mainstream lifestyle with a husband, two kids, a dog, and four cats. Then the rug that was my life got pulled out from under me. One day, my former husband—the one I thought was my person, the one who I thought would love me forever—unceremoniously told me that he didn't love me anymore and couldn't remember when he did love me.

What did he say?

Did I mention that—to add insult to injury—this was the year I turned fifty years old? Oh, and I was also going through menopause, and my two teenage daughters were going through puberty. In retrospect, this might not seem too earth-shattering, especially when you read about the experiences others have lived. But for me, *it was huge!*

This experience exposed some deep wounds that I had very neatly covered up. In fact, it ripped the scabs right off my wounds, and I quickly sank into a depression. Yet all these experiences combined became my agent for change. They sent me searching for deeper answers and ultimately sent me on my journey of spiritual transformation.

What has sustained me through all of it is my unwavering knowing that I am Spirit.

We can move beyond the suffering and the doubt that life changes create. When we see the changes not as lessons or punishments, but as opportunities to experience emotion, our awareness expands. Changes become possibilities for growth and service. Our confidence increases and our wounding patterns heal. Our self-talk changes from "Why me?" or "What's wrong with me?" to "I got this!" and "How can I help?"

When we know deep down in the core of our being that we are Spirit, the chaos clears. As Spirit, we are not small. Our lives have a purpose, and we are embraced and supported by the Divine Oneness of which we, and all of life, are a part.

To support you on our beautiful, collective journey, I offer a part of my sacred story. This experience gave me a glimmer of understanding of the support we have and our interconnectedness to all.

Wisdom from the Whale

I was blessed for eighteen years to live in a home whose backyard is protected by a large rock face. The rock looks like a gigantic whale that is forever floating, watching, and recording life and the endless cycles that play out before it. I had spent many happy times gazing at it and wondering about life's mysteries. What has that gigantic rock seen through the eons that it has stood, steadfast, as the silent observer? What secrets could it tell?

But the whale also offered me a personal struggle. For in the contours of the whale's belly and fin, weeds grew, and those weeds distracted me and upset my peace and calm. I could easily pluck out the weeds growing near the bottom of the rock face, restoring my whale to its unfettered self, but I had a hard time reaching the weeds that were higher up.

For years, I struggled with this. When I was married, I would ask my husband to climb up and pull them for me, as I was afraid to climb the rock myself. A few times over the years, when I could no longer wait for my husband to do it, I would attempt that climb. Then I would get stuck, halfway up the rock face, afraid to move, frozen in panic. My fear of heights would engulf me, and I would scream for my children to come to my rescue, to offer me their hands and help me back down to safety.

Forever optimistic or possibly obstinate, one day, I decided to try again. As a living being, the rock face was always slightly changing; parts of it periodically loosened and crumbled to the ground below, making the climb a slightly different challenge each time. On this day, I approached the whale and found footing a couple of feet up.

Maybe I can reach the weeds from here, I thought, and I stretched and strained to reach the little plants that had grown too high up. However, as in all the times past, the weeds were still beyond my reach. To make matters worse, this time, the footing I was on did not feel secure. I realized I needed to take another step up or make my way back down, defeated once again. But I was determined to succeed, so I looked around to find a better foothold. A few feet above me, I spied what seemed to be solid footing. If I could get to the next step, I'd be able to reach the weeds above.

I centered myself and went inward for strength, knowing this was about more than pulling weeds. I thought about the journey I had lived so far—the changes in my life that I had experienced and the wisdom and courage I had gained. Through it all, I was reminded that I am a spiritual being, and I am part of the Oneness that is all around us. This Oneness includes nature and all living beings, seen and unseen.

I knew at that moment that I would not fall.

I knew I was supported and loved and protected by the Divine Oneness, including my special friend, the whale. For the first time in eighteen years,

I was going to reach the unreachable weeds, and in pulling them, take a giant step forward in my healing.

I relaxed into that knowing, and I stepped up. My new footing was secure—in fact, much more secure than the place I'd been standing. I had to laugh as I received great clarity. In life, we only need to trust. Relax into and trust the Divine Oneness. With a smile on my face and peace in my heart I pulled the weeds and climbed back down without assistance. As I stood on the ground, I looked up at the newly groomed whale and gave thanks for the gift received.

And in the next step, the struggle lessens.

As we move forward on our journeys, and our awareness expands to include the depth of who we are, our footing becomes more secure. Often it is easier to take the next step and move forward than to stretch and strain from a place that no longer serves us.

Relax into your knowing and trust. As you begin to thoughtfully practice your trust, the gifts from the experience of change emerge.

Take the next step with us.

On our journeys, we don't need to have everything figured out. We only need to take the next step, secure in the knowledge that we are loved and supported. Join us as we travel together through these heart-opening and heartbreaking stories of change. May you laugh and may you cry, for in the experience is the emotion, and in the emotion is the gift.

Much love,

Patricia

The Psychology of Change

by Kathleen O'Keefe-Kanavos

Change can bring with it a deluge of emotions,
from sadness to clarity—and, finally, gratitude.

Welcome to true-life stories about change and its human connection to worldwide Oneness. The Global Voice of authors who dared to bare their souls and report on their darkest hours—and the times chaos changed into defining moments of clarity—is a gift to all who seek solace from life's challenges. I am eternally grateful for their unfettered honesty. Their journeys are Joseph Campbell's "The Hero's Journey." In my opinion, every author in this book is a hero.

All the stories are from the personal experiences of people around the world. These tales are built on the complexities of the multiple layers of real life. The stories are not cookie-cutter health stories or love sagas. They cross boundaries that are blurred by reality, and they are spoken with a global voice. They reflect our Universal connection to life, emotion, and thought, and depict our natural desire to overcome crisis and emerge from the conflicted storms of life physically and mentally intact—and grateful.

Chaos Theory is a part of mathematics that describes certain systems as very sensitive; therefore, a very small change might make a system behave differently. Life is sensitive. One aspect of Chaos Theory is the so-called "Butterfly Effect," which states that even the flapping of a tiny butterfly wing can create enough wind to change weather patterns around the world. Science might not be able to measure how much change will result from the flapping of the small wings, but science can indisputably predict that change will be a result. It is cause and effect in motion. Change creates change.

Even a very small shift in initial conditions will create a significantly different outcome.

What this means is when a butterfly beats its wings, the airflow affected around it will be indirectly felt on the other side of the world, because everything on Earth is interconnected.

Another way to explain the effect of change is the example of a pebble dropped into a still pool of water. The pebble creates ripples that will affect the edges of the pool, no matter how far away they might be. Multiple stones make ripples that interconnect, creating shared space.

Imagine the stories in this book are pebbles in the pool of human consciousness. The rapid heartbeats from lessons learned can be compared to the beating butterfly wings of change. A sigh from a reader becomes the wind beneath its wings. A story that touches the mind of one reader creates ripples that touch the edges of humanity through Universal awareness. If one reader can create a ripple effect, imagine how multiple readers can create intersecting rings in Universal Consciousness. Therefore, according to the mathematically proven Chaos Theory, by reading these stories, you have the potential to be a part of world change.

If you think of the book as a magic carpet ride, one strong common thread of change woven throughout its tapestry is the unselfish hope of helping others who may still be on their life's Hero's Journey. We can see this in Helen Brennand's story about the death of her infant son. Death can herald a coming-of-age change, as seen in my mother's death and in the grief and loss experienced by the other authors. Death is the ultimate life-changer. But, as so many stories share, love never dies. Like the circle of life, the circle of love remains eternally unbroken.

♪Love is a Many Splendored Thing … or so the 1955 song goes, until it isn't. And truth be told, who wants to live in a world without love, or without the hope of ever finding love again? Divorce is often seen as a psychological death, causing many of the symptoms of severe grief. Yet after the painful life-lesson of lost love, we can find love again—no matter how wrong they may seem at the time, like Denise Alexander Pyle, and at any age, like Lynn Forrester. These stories are a breath of fresh air.

Cassandra Tindal's story exemplifies the psychological importance of the need to be heard and accepted as being worthy of love, especially as a child. The habit of suppressed emotions can be deadly.

Humans are creatures of habit. Our traditions and rituals bring us a sense of comfort and emotional security in our habits. When we change, the results can be devastating to an individual, group, culture, or planet. Yet we know physical and psychological change is inevitable.

Every new thing learned creates a psychological change. Some of our physical body cells change daily. Change does not have to be painful or frightening. When accepted as the natural flow of life on Earth, even death can be embraced as an opportunity for growth.

Earth is a fickle home. Change in the form of floods, volcanic eruptions, strikes by giant meteors from space, and drastic climate changes can test the adaptability of physical and emotional change on a species. The bones of dinosaurs attest to this fact.

Without the ability to adapt to and embrace change, there is no hope for a future.

The emotional symptom of change is often stress, which can make you feel like pulling out your hair—although occasionally, it falls out on its own. Glenda-Ray Riviere writes about a stress-related condition known as *telogen effluvium*, a form of temporary hair loss that usually happens after a shock or traumatic event. It occurs when a large number of hairs enter into a resting phase while the body and psyche overcome a stressful change or situation. Telogen effluvium is different from the drug-related alopecia I experienced during chemotherapy.

The stress of change can also lead to cravings, which began with early Man's first food binges and continues with junk food today. According to Dr. Leigh Gibson of the University of Roehampton[1], "We're programmed to eat fatty and sugary substances during stress that began during the time of caveman." Cravings happen when the brain's opioid and dopamine react to the benefit of high-caloric- food as a fight-or-flight survival mechanism, or a kick-start out of depression. Kristi Tornabene's story of being repeatedly told "You're fat!" is a hero's journey to overcome eating habits, despite her genetic tendencies, so she could fit into her favorite jeans again. Name-calling hurts. Sticks and stones may break our bones, but names will break our hearts or even shatter our minds.

Our minds are our invisible brain, and our brain is our body's master computer that alerts us to physical and emotional changes. We often communicate with ourselves about change through dreams and nightmares. Our dreams are more than the random firings of a sleeping brain. According to the research in the book *Dreams That Can Save Your Life*[2], co-authored by Kathleen O'Keefe-Kanavos and radiologist Dr. Larry Burk of Duke University Medical, dreams can be early warning signs of disease.

Dreams can be a microcosm of our daily life, or as in the case of Kathleen O'Keefe-Kanavos' story and that of Tamee Knox, an answer to important information about a health crisis. A deceased loved one spoke to Tammy in her dreams. Kathleen heard from Franciscan monks. Persistent dreams like these, when validated by medical tests, can change and save lives.

Challenges often present themselves as opportunities for change, and change can be the ultimate challenge. The thirty authors in this book share how they suffered tears of rage, sadness, fear, and joy. Their eventual change created a life where they now live in joy. They have left the suffering behind.

Author Gina Roda said to me in a phone call, "Writing my story on change created a huge breakthrough in my life. I've always wanted to write but never could complete what I started. I feel so good! This has never happened to me before." Change is powerful!

I went through breast cancer treatment while still grieving the death of my mother, who had died of colon cancer. The most life-changing lesson I learned was that it is human to be in physical pain, but emotional suffering is a choice. It is all a matter of perception. When I changed my thought process, it changed my life. If I did not *mind* it (take it into my psyche), it did not *matter* (manifest.)

These are easy words to mouth, but they can be hard to live; however, we must start somewhere. Even reading the words can lead to the beginning of change. This is the Butterfly Effect in action.

Enjoy your magic carpet ride. And thank you for being one of the ripples of change.

PART 1

LOVE AND RELATIONSHIPS
Crazy Little Thing Called Love

Listen to the voices
that sing remembrances
to your soul

Message Received
by Rev. Patricia Cagganello

You are lovable. Just breathe.

Life can be funny, in a twisted sort of way. The year I celebrated my fiftieth birthday, I got divorced, went through menopause, and battled depression, while being a single mom to my two hormonal teenage daughters. To tell you it was easy would be silly. I was hanging on by a thread.

Once I stopped mourning the loss of my relationship with my ex-husband, I focused on recovering a healthy relationship with myself. However, it seemed that any self-love or self-esteem I was trying to establish was blown away with even the slightest amount of teenage angst my daughters directed my way. Normal adolescent behaviors—like rolled eyes, a tone of voice, correcting me, wanting to hang out with their friends instead of me, and even not cleaning their rooms—would send me into a tailspin.

To say I was sensitive would be a gross understatement. I took everything my girls did personally. Every word or action was a specific judgment of my value and the ability for someone to love me.

You are lovable. Just breathe.

"Patience, patience, patience," I would tell myself. "Just breathe. Don't take things so personally. Slow down. You are lovable. Just breathe."

But relentless waves of emotional challenges kept getting in my way. Arguments with my girls erupted almost daily. They said I was moody and hard to deal with. They felt I was picking on them. But to me, they seemed insensitive and self-centered.

We had more "start overs" than we could count, our way to deal with disagreements or misunderstandings. In the past, we'd been able to release any lingering blame or hard feelings and move forward simply by agreeing to a start over. This strategy worked great when they were little, but eventually, even a start over couldn't fix things.

My girls kept trying, though. They saw the mother that they had always known changing and their support, their foundation, cracking. I know it scared them; it scared me. They reached out to me in their own ways, trying to help me. They fought to restore some semblance of normalcy in their lives.

Battling my own thoughts, perceptions, and feelings was the hardest thing I had ever done.

Each morning, I woke up and resolved to make it a better day. It was going to be a kinder and gentler day, not only for me but for my girls. I would be calm, nice, and less critical.

Sometimes this happened—but most days, I would see myself and the people around me through my distorted lens of emotion. I would take offense. My feelings would be hurt, and I'd lash out with wounded and angry words. Most nights, I went to bed deflated and mad at myself, resolving once again that I'd do better the next day.

My older daughter would challenge me and question my behaviors and emotions. Seeing my weaknesses unnerved her. She wanted to see my strength, wanted me to fight. What she didn't realize was that I was fighting.

We both knew the script by heart; our disagreements seemed unending. We were like two performers in a play, forever acting out our roles, performance after performance, in a drama that should have long closed.

But my daughter's capacity to love is boundless, her capacity to forgive is great, and her resolve is strong. Even after the worst disagreements, she would always come to find me, to try and make it right.

"Mom, I love you!" she would say. "I'm sorry."

"I don't believe you," was my typical reply, as I turned my face away from her. Too hurt and ashamed to look her in the eye.

"Mom, look at me! I mean it. I love you, and I don't want to fight."

"I don't know what to do," I would sob, truly at a loss.

"We love you. You have to believe me. It's going to be ok," she would promise as she reached over to hug me.

"I love you and I'm sorry too," I assured her, overcome with remorse, hugging her back and praying my reactions would improve.

One day during this stretch, I had retreated to my bedroom after a particularly bruising confrontation.

I had needed a break, just for a few minutes, to calm down. That was my new strategy: I'd remove myself from the argument before it escalated. I began to pace the floor, trying to clear my head.

One of my favorite things about my bedroom is that it looks out over "the cliff," which is a giant slab of rock that runs parallel to our back patio.

The rock is sixty feet wide and boasts a steep, twenty-foot drop at its highest point.

From my bedroom window, the rock face seems to resemble a giant whale. I have always imagined how it has floated through time, calmly and lovingly observing generations of all species, and how it holds untold history and knowledge in its unwavering, all-encompassing gaze. The cliff is a striking backdrop in our yard, and I have spent many hours admiring and breathing in its majestic presence.

That day, I paced back and forth, too upset to do more than glance at the landscape. But after a few minutes, something caught my eye. I paused and peered out the window. It was a deer—a large mother deer— standing on the apex of the rock. It looked like she was listening for something. Her head was tilted upward. *How pretty*, I thought, and began pacing again. We see deer all the time in our area, so it didn't hold my attention.

A short time later, I noticed that the deer was still there. She hadn't moved, from what I could tell. Her head was still pointed to the sky, as if she was entranced by some distant star. The pose was unusual – it no longer seemed like she was listening for something. Her ears weren't twitching, and she hadn't moved her head. Yet I still wasn't sure this was odd behavior for a female deer. *Maybe she's just standing watch*, I thought. *Maybe her young are playing just beyond the edge of the rock.*

I quickly became engrossed in my thoughts again, mentally replaying the argument I'd had with one of my girls. She had left me a little annoyed with her actions, but mostly, I felt guilty for fighting with her. I regretted putting more strain on our relationship.

Ten minutes or so must have passed before I out the window again. The deer was still standing in the same position, as if frozen in time. I did a double take. *What was she still doing there?*

I trained my eyes and really focused on the deer for the first time and was immediately struck by how beautiful she was. The best word I can think of to describe her is "regal." She exuded a tranquil presence.

She had a white underbelly that led to the rich, caramel-colored fur that covered most of her body. Her face was a mask of white accents in graceful symmetry. Her ears were outlined in light gray fur. A long, snowy rectangle sprouted at the base of her chin and curved downwards to the middle of her neck. Her shiny black eyes and nose rested in pockets of white. Her deep, wise eyes were clearly visible.

The deer stood atop the rock as if it were a throne, as if God had made this royal mantle the place where she had been born to stand. My eyes lingered on her for a moment longer as I took in this powerful sight.

I stepped away from the window, shaking my head, feeling genuinely lucky to have witnessed the presence of this wonderful mother deer. I couldn't believe she had stayed still for so long, with her head held high.

'Wait a minute. I raced back to the window, but the deer was gone. Of course, she was gone.

She had a message for me, and I had finally gotten it.

Female deer are graceful creatures, never aggressive to humans or other animals. Deer are herbivores that eat vegetation: nuts, seeds, fruits, and often the flowers from your favorite plants. The females are mostly seen as they quietly travel with one or two other female deer and their fawns. It is so unusual to hear a deer make a sound that most people couldn't describe the sound they make.

Because of these characteristics, deer are associated with gentleness. The message of a deer is to be kind and gentle with yourself. After a visit from a deer, an opportunity might present itself for you to be kind and gentle to others, and that might open up new possibilities for you. The deer's appearance asks you whether you're being too critical with yourself.

Did this apply to me? Was I critical with myself, feeling I couldn't do anything right? Yes!

Was I kind and gentle to others? No, not on most days—especially not to my girls.

The fact that the deer was standing on the top of my very large rock face also seemed symbolic. A rocky landscape is symbolic of sturdiness and steadfastness. An animal standing on a high perch, as the deer was, also indicates looking at things from a different perspective.

I needed a different perspective.

The deer was standing perfectly still. She was pausing. Perhaps she was my reminder to really pause, breathe, and be gentle with myself and others. Her visit encouraged me to try to look at things from a perspective that was different from the one racing through my head.

Mom we love you. You have to believe us.

My daughter's words echoed. Yes, I could be kinder and gentler to myself and my girls. Just pause and breathe. Don't take things so personally. Believe in their love.

This time, I was not only fighting for my girls; I had to fight for myself. With new clarity, and feeling support from our animal friends, I knew that this time, I could do it.

This story appears in Patricia's first book *God is in the Little Things: Messages from the Animals.*

They Are Coming Home
by Anrita Melchizedek

The timeless, eternal NOW moment, where all is love.
For truly, love is all there is.

I was completely alone, save for my fifteen-month-old, teething toddler in the next room. I didn't feel quite prepared for this birth but wanted to honor the natural rhythm of my body. The contractions grew stronger and more uncomfortable. Lying in the bath, I breathed deeply and counted the seconds between contractions, hoping these were Braxton Hicks contractions—practice contractions to remind my body of the imminent birth. But then the pain intensified. I was in labor—alone, and two weeks earlier than anticipated.

This was my second birth, and I attuned naturally to the rhythm of my body while focusing on the beautiful soul choosing to have me as its mother in this lifetime. This baby's energy had been felt powerfully three to four months previously, appearing in my meditation. I remembered the delight of merging with this celestial soul—the familiarity and deep sense of love.

I hoped this soul would have less karma to unravel in clearing and dissolving lower timelines. The vision of our lifetimes together—as lovers and friends, priests and priestesses, healers and monks—played like a movie screen on fast-forward with no sound.

When I thought of my husband, my breathing changed. I was glad he was not here.

Ours had been the complicated, karmic relationship of the narcissist and empath. Finally, tired of the victim/persecutor consciousness roles we had chosen, with the accompanying fighting, shouting, and abuse, I'd decided on divorce, but knew it was not yet the right time.

I had recently returned to Cape Town, after a year in Lisbon with my husband, to have a home birth. At the time, home births were not available in Portugal. My husband had given me six months to return. I knew I would never return as his wife.

The cries of my fifteen-month-old teething toddler brought my attention back to this moment and the realization that there were no adults in the house to help me give birth. My child's back teeth were coming in, and he was running a fever. When his crying escalated, I quickly got out of the bath and put on my dressing gown. I needed to pick up my toddler, to apply more teething gel on his sore gums and again take his temperature. It was still rather high. I gave him paracetamol syrup for the pain and fever and hoped he would go back to sleep.

I walked around with my toddler on my right hip, trying to continue my deep breathing and call the midwife who had delivered my first child. I'd been in labor seventy-two hours with him before my home water birth and cringed at the thought of going through that again! My call went to voicemail. It was around ten p.m. on a windy night in Cape Town, South Africa, where blustery weather conditions often weakened the mobile phone signals. My calls were not going through.

The midwife was staying in a remote area with bad cell phone reception.

After sending a text message, I prepared to give birth alone. Candles and gentle background music created a calm atmosphere as I rocked my toddler. The contractions shot a brief, sharp spasm of pain through my lower abdomen and back.

I had not seen a gynecologist in Portugal. Being comfortable with my body had convinced me I didn't need medical intervention. Now my deep breathing lulled me into a deep, trance-like state. If the midwife did not arrive in time, I would be fine.

My phone started to ring at about three a.m. The midwife was on her way. By then, I had been in labor for five and a half hours.

Fighting against the wild wind as my contractions increased, I hurried to open the wooden side gate for the midwife, who arrived thirty minutes later. I put the kettle on for us, and then she checked my cervical dilation. I had hoped for another home water birth, but the midwife told me the baby would be born soon. It was too late for a water birth. I settled on a horseshoe-shaped, wooden birth seat that would allow me to comfortably squat and give birth.

My water broke and I vomited twice. This baby was about to arrive.

Squatting, I lifted my gown to my waist and vocalized in deep, primordial groans as the baby's head peeked out from my vagina. With another deep push and groan, out came a beautiful baby boy. After the midwife cut the umbilical cord and wiped him down, I took him in my arms and helped his mouth find one of my breasts. He started to suck, gently at first, and then with a more confident latch.

The love in the room was palpable. *This is truly heaven on Earth*, I thought, smiling broadly at the midwife. I loved being a mother, although being on my own was hard work with a toddler and my own consulting work.

My husband arrived two weeks after the birth and stayed for two weeks before returning to Portugal. He knew I was not ready to return to Portugal, and we arranged for him to spend a couple of weeks in South Africa every four months.

We would not be staying together permanently. Even our short time together, along with our daily Skype sessions, created a great deal of inner torment. Our relationship worsened. A couple of months after my baby's first birthday, I asked for a divorce.

He surprised me by being amicable to the idea of divorce. Since we had been married in South Africa, he returned to the Sheriff's Court and signed the divorce papers so I could complete the proceedings through the High Court. Waiting for the High Court in Cape Town, I reflected on the past four years, and how he had changed shortly after we married.

He had become jealous, possessive, controlling, and judgmental.

Portugal had been a lonely time for me, as he had often left me in the house while he went out on his own. His name-calling, shouting, and shaming created a chaotic and miserable environment.

But now there was a light at the end of the tunnel. At three and five years old, my boys had unique and amazing personalities. My oldest loved to dance and I would often dance with them around the house, with my baby swinging from my hip and my older son dancing by my side or balanced on my other hip.

I moved into a new rental, but the relationship with my ex-husband changed very little. Knowing it was important for the children to have their father in their lives, I stepped back from our disagreements as much as possible. Finally, I no longer wanted him staying in my house when he came to visit. The disharmony when we were together affected the children, too.

And, he started to bring his girlfriend, later to become his third wife, along on visits. I found the courage to tell them to find their own holiday accommodation and to take the children with them for the weeks they were in Cape Town. This made him angry. But I hadn't realized how much he resented or perhaps even hated me.

They came out again in August 2012 to take the boys for a ten-day holiday. As I packed their bags, we all felt the excitement. My children would have a holiday with their dad, and I'd have some time for myself. Waving goodbye left me feeling slightly anxious, but I wasn't sure why. We had agreed I would call daily and for the first few days, all seemed well.

Five days later, I was not able to reach them.

My ex-husband's home phone had been turned off, and so had his international mobile. I continued to call with growing panic, afraid there had been an accident. The next day, I reported my concern to the police. Two days later, my ex sent me a text message saying he had taken the boys to Portugal.

He had organized Portuguese passports at the consulate in Cape Town, and with his girlfriend, had passed through international customs. Seven months prior, he had stopped paying monthly child support and had presented me instead with an agreement for financial assistance. This would help him receive financial aid from the Portuguese government. I had not realized he would use this to claim I neither cared for the children nor was able to provide any income to support them. He also had opened a case with the Family Court in Portugal prior to coming to South Africa stating I was an unfit mother. He claimed I was a drug addict and alcoholic who had sexually abused the children, locked them up, and beaten them.

He had abducted my children.

How could this have happened? It felt like the plot of someone else's movie. My babies were gone. Although I called daily, almost a year passed before I spoke to the boys on the telephone. I felt the angels telling me to trust in the process and reassuring me that the highest good would prevail. I tried to surrender to this process, but my grief was overwhelming.

I researched my options for child abduction cases and was advised to take my complaint to the High Court in South Africa. In December 2012, the High Court in Cape Town ruled the children must be returned to South Africa. I traveled to Portugal with the High Court Order, only to discover the order was not recognized in Portugal.

Some months later, the National Central Authorities in Portugal ordered the Family Court to return the children to South Africa—but the Family Court refused, based on their father's testimony of abuse. They would need written testimony from the South African courts attesting to my character.

As my court case took shape in Portugal, I submitted to psychological evaluations, social worker evaluations, court appearances, and legal meetings. My friends in Cape Town provided testimony on my behalf.

Almost three years passed. I came to forgive my ex-husband for what he had done to me, but it took much longer to forgive him for what he had done to the boys. The few times I was able to speak on the phone with my eldest son, he had shouted about imaginary abuse, spurred on by his father. Their confusion and sense of abandonment broke my heart into tiny pieces. I knew how they felt; their confusion, their issues of abandonment.

I would never stop fighting for them, no matter how long it took.

Then it happened. I was able to walk in my ex-husband's shoes through the heart of compassion, to understand his pain: his father's early death, being sent to boarding school when his mom remarried. His childhood had lacked love. His arrogance stemmed from a sense of inferiority and being unseen and unheard.

I recognized that we'd had an agreement, prior to incarnating, to play out the victim-persecutor consciousness roles. The goal was to come to know ourselves as love. Love was revealed in all its facets. I forgave him and released blame.

My heart told me the children would soon be coming home to me. Within a week, one of the social workers called to say, "They are coming home. Your children are coming home. The Family Court in Portugal has released the boys into your custody."

"They are coming home," I repeated. "They are coming home." I smiled with the wisdom of experience and the stillness of a loving heart. Many lower timelines, karmic timelines, dissolved.

Back in South Africa with my boys, I offered a path of reconciliation to my ex-husband with a parental agreement in which he could be a regular part of their lives, but I did not hear back from him.

The highest outcome had prevailed.

What I see clearly now is that I chose this experience, as we all did. I am grateful for being able to pass through the karmic timelines and enter the Portal of Divine Love—the timeless, eternal *Now* moment, where all is love. For truly, love is all there is.

Courage Is Fear That Said Its Prayers
by Teresa Velardi

Never let anyone steal your joy.

Who are you and why are you here? I demanded, sobbing as I gazed at myself in the mirror.

It had been a long time since I'd looked myself in the eye. With tears streaming down my face from swollen eyes, it was difficult to recognize myself. It wasn't just the tears that had me wondering who the stranger in the mirror was. It was the lack of life, the long-lost joy, and the missing smile that made me ask those tough questions.

That was my "come to Jesus" moment. You know the one I mean.

It was the moment I finally got real about life, my authentic self, and God.

My two-fold question had to be answered from two perspectives. "Who are you?" I had become completely lost in the insanity of my marriage to an abusive, alcoholic, drug-addicted man. Everything I'd once loved had been sacrificed in the name of love: my art, my writing, my friends. Everything was now under his control. Without realizing it, I had utterly abandoned myself and my power. Even my perspective on what it meant to be a good mother to my young son was lost. We weren't safe.

That led to, "Why are you here?" The answer scared me. I didn't know how to get out and was overwhelmed with fear—afraid for my life, my sanity, and my child.

My answers to those questions needed to come from a higher perspective. Who did God create me to be, and what was my purpose in life? I had no clue how to answer either of those important questions—just the desire to find out!

For nearly fifteen years leading up to that moment, I'd lived a "scripted life." There was never any hope of my dreams coming true, because someone else had become the center of my every day. It seemed as if my life didn't matter. I'll admit, at times, I believed it to be true.

If not for my son, I might not have lived to tell the story of breaking free from a life of unimportance.

My life was controlled by manipulation, codependence, and deceit.

Would life have been different without the drugs and alcohol that seemed to consume every waking moment of my husband's existence? Was I dealing with who he truly was, or with an alter-ego created by the effects of the substances? There was no way to know. I only knew I was living with Dr. Jekyll and Mr. Hyde.

I kept telling myself, "He said he was gonna stop being verbally abusive, yet he's doing it again. It must be the alcohol and drugs talking. That's not really who he is—is it?"

With every critical moment that came and went, his promises to change his ways evaporated. It made no sense for me to believe he would honor the promise he'd made to stop drinking and drugging when we got married. So why had I ever believed that lie?

I stood at the altar before the priest who had married my parents more than a quarter of a century before.

The limousine had been tardy to pick me up. That was the first thing that went wrong. I arrived at the church for my wedding nearly an hour late. Although I didn't realize it then, God had put up a huge roadblock. The Long Island Expressway traffic kept the limo from getting me to the church on time. It's no coincidence that the roadway is called the LIE, because my life became just that—a LIE!

My father had doubled up on his dental appointments the previous day so he could look his very best as he walked me down the aisle. As Dad handed me over to my soon-to-be husband, I was overcome by a sinking feeling of dread. Gazing lovingly into my groom's eyes, I could see that he was high as a kite.

He couldn't even keep his promise to be sober when we took our vows!

For a fleeting moment, I thought about running. I gave my future husband a look of disappointment that said, "Really?"

Why did I go through with the wedding? I was more concerned about what everyone else in the church would think if I were to hightail it out of there, with my dress flapping in the wind, than what I would think of myself if I did not run from this mistake. However, obstacle number two was quickly swept under the rug.

Then the priest read the wrong passages. After all the time I'd spent choosing the perfect words for my wedding, I was left with a puzzled look on my face. The groom could not have cared less. Another thing had gone wrong. What else could possibly happen on this most important day of my life?

Our vows were next. The groom said his vows first, and then it was my turn. The priest asked, "Teresa, do you take this man to be your wedded husband …"

As the priest was reading the words, I was staring at the kite flying high in the eyes of the groom. My heart spoke: *Teresa, don't do this.* It stopped me cold.

I looked around the room at all my family and friends who had gathered to witness that very special moment. The *voice* was probably just the stress of having been late, I figured—and the disappointment of seeing my groom high. I later came to believe it was the voice of God directing me to a different future, which began with me running like hell out of that church. But I stood in silence, trying to talk my way out of listening.

How could I leave the altar when my father looked so proud? My future mother-in-law was dressed to the nines. I looked at my mother. She knew. She could see I was having second thoughts.

The priest began again. "Teresa, do you take this man …"

Again, I heard, *Teresa, don't do this. I have someone so much better for you.*

Once again, I froze, looking around the room. How could I walk away from all these people? I caved. "I do," I whispered, and as the words left my lips, my heart fell to my feet.

At that moment, I'd sold my soul for a wedding band. And that was just the beginning.

After the thrill of the wedding wore off, I was left with day-to-day life with a man more married to bottles of booze and pills than he ever was to me. The more he drank, the nastier he became.

Although he seemed delighted when he found out he was going to be a father, he declared the baby would be a boy and they would do their best to "gang up on me." Who says something like that?

We attended a wedding where he served as a groomsman, and I watched him cast me aside. He was more interested in the bridesmaid he was paired with than he was in me. While he told the bartender to keep my glass of ginger ale full, I recognized the evidence of his cheating heart. Infidelity was a regular part of my too-many years of marriage.

I did my best to make my son my top priority, even knowing his young eyes and ears were witnessing far too much verbal, emotional, and soon, physical abuse. He developed behavioral issues. His father would tell him, "Don't listen to your mother. She doesn't know what she's talking about," teaching him to defy me. By the time he was six, child psychologists had diagnosed him with something called "oppositional defiant disorder." The diagnosis spoke for itself.

Our son was not a good sleeper. His internal clock kept him awake all night, so getting him up for school on time was a daily nightmare. His father was no help because he was out every night doing his thing. Although still married, I felt like a single parent.

I felt like God was punishing me for not listening to him at the altar. I'd grown up in a household where God was depicted as punishing and vengeful, so I was afraid to call upon Him now to help me. Even though church on Sundays was still a part of my life, I felt spiritually bankrupt.

It was time to change the focus of what had become a pathetic life. I knew I needed to focus on me—to find my joy again, my smile, and the light in my eyes. In my heart, and the depths of my broken soul, I knew I'd never find joy inside this marriage of madness!

A friend invited me to Al-Anon, a 12-step program for friends and families of alcoholics.

The meetings taught me how to shift my focus away from the insanity of the alcoholic and concentrate on how to be a better me and a better mother to my son.

As I began making myself a priority and talking about what was going on in my life, a heaviness was lifted off my shoulders. The reassurance and support of the friends made in Al-Anon kept me hopeful that my life could change. Gradually, it did—but not before I had to go to court several times for orders of protection, when things got really bad.

While I was taking control of my life, my husband was spiraling downward, often losing his temper and taking it out on me. When he threatened to kill me, I left my home and went into hiding with my son.

Anticipating my husband's every step was a full-time job. One day, he tried to kidnap my son from school. I'd had the foresight to leave a copy of an order of protection at the school, prohibiting him from doing that. The law student who had helped me in court said the judge would never include that clause, but I'd dared to explain to the judge that because my husband was addicted to pain pills, the people at the school might not recognize that he was under the influence. Luckily, the judge had agreed with me.

Now, here we are, many years later. My ex-husband is out of my life. My son is successful and passionate about what he does, and he lives nearby. I'm grateful that I get to be an example of what it means to live an abundant life full of blessings, healthy relationships, spiritual well-being, and emotional health—each worth more than financial abundance.

They say courage is fear that said its prayers.

I learned to flex my courage muscle, big time! I did my best by trying to stand up for myself in every fearful situation until it became my way of life. And, I was never alone on the journey. After believing God had abandoned me and was punishing me for so long, I finally found my way back to Him, and I've let Him guide my every step.

It has not always been easy, but my struggle brought me closer to becoming the woman I was created to be. God loves me more than I can imagine. He protects me, brings the right people to me, and guides me to abundant life. He also has a great sense of humor. It is through Him that all things are possible—and once again, I can laugh and be joyful.

Never let anyone steal your joy!

A Badass Butterfly Conversion: A Woman's Liberation

by Dr. Jane Galloway

My life changed forever, one day at a time.

It only took a moment! And it wasn't a "rock" bottom, but more like a trampoline bounce.

The first time I attended an AA meeting, I was beat—out of good ideas, depressed, adrift, and physically and emotionally sick. I still worked in the New York theatre and appeared on television regularly—and occasionally on the *New York Post*'s famous Page-Six gossip column—but I was plummeting toward a deep abyss of despair and addiction.

I could not stop drinking and using stimulant drugs to keep me going.

My emotional development had been arrested at sixteen—the age when I picked up my first addictive substance. For at least ten years, my emotional self was pretty much stuck there—but my life went on. My personality was shaped by addiction, social norms, and fear of rejection. All of which was kept in a kind of suspended reality by using whatever substance (or behavior, or both) would rescue me from feeling the agony I was trying to avoid.

Amphetamine diet pills had succeeded in controlling my weight, and in my industry, being thin was a ticket to work. But as a side effect of the diet pills, I didn't feel psychological pain—as long as I could keep from "coming down." Fear of facing the pain under the addiction kept me going and going, until I broke.

The problem with self-prescribed drug therapy is that the body develops a tolerance to these substances, and increasing doses are necessary to get the same result. Eventually, the medication becomes the problem, when years of buried pain can't be suppressed anymore.

If we're lucky, we plunge to the bottom and seek treatment. People who moralize about drugs don't understand this basic truth: Addiction is pain control. Becoming addicted is the unfortunate by-product of a strategy that starts out as a self-help survival tool.

A bounce into another dimension.

But my bottom was not a "rock" bottom, a land of broken things. It was a moment of utter, existential aloneness followed by a cosmic intervention and a trampoline bounce into a whole different life.

I hit that bottom very late one night. My first love had just told me he was marrying someone else. It wasn't like he had spontaneously made this decision without trying to engage me in meaningful conversation about our relationship. He had tried hard. But I'd been unable to show up for that conversation.

I now know that we were not the right life match, and maybe I even knew it then, but I wasn't ready to face it. This particular Monday evening, he came over for dinner, as he did many Monday evenings, but this time, he told me he was getting married. I went into shock and started talking really fast. I can't remember how I made it through the rest of the evening, but, copious amounts of scotch were involved.

When he left my apartment, I was stone-cold sober, in spite of having drunk half a fifth of scotch. This is an awful hell beyond words and is just one of the symptoms of developing tolerance. In the stillness of my Greenwich Village apartment, I experienced an existential void and true despair beyond description.

At that moment, I "saw" myself at the center of a circle of isolation I had created. I had pushed everyone I knew cared for me out of my life, and had one horrible, timeless moment of living hell. It is hard to fully describe, but it was a moment of the deepest despair, depression, physical drunkenness, and existential emptiness I had ever experienced or ever wish to experience again. I was utterly alone in the Universe.

At that moment a brilliant white Light came into the room, and a voice came with it. I know Light isn't supposed to talk, but this one actually did. I was lying in bed, pretending to read a book, sipping expensive brandy, and free-falling into the void. And then time stopped. The room was suffused with a bright white Light, a peaceful hum, and this white talking Light said, "It's over. It's the drinking."

And it was. It was over, thank God. This moment was what I think is meant by Grace. Something came to get me from the pit of despair, and the next day, I began a whole different life. Well, I was actually sick as a dog and hung over, and THEN I started a whole new life.

One more supernatural experience was still to come.

At my first 12-Step meeting, later that very day, I told the people about the Light. To my great surprise, many of them nodded their heads in recognition. It was amazing. They knew what I was talking about. Some version of the Light must have come to get them, too.

And something else happened at that meeting. I was sitting quietly, all dressed up, certain nobody could tell I was an alcoholic. It seems laughable now, but we cling to our illusions. I *inhaled* the meeting, soaking up these people's experiences, and I saw myself in every one of their stories. Toward the end of the meeting, the leader looked right at me and said, "Young lady, would you like to share with us?"

I couldn't believe it. Just to show you how crazy I really was, my first thought was: *Oh, they probably think I am from the New York Times and writing a story about AA.*

Out of touch, you say? Grandiose? Just a bit. But something in me knew that if I did not make my way to the front of that basement room, I might never go back. It was a matter of my life and death.

When I got to the front of the room, my mouth began to move, and I heard "My name is Jane, and I'm an alcoholic."

The next second my entire life to date flashed before my eyes. It's difficult to explain, but this amazing experience lasted just a few seconds in real time. It was like experiencing a death and reincarnation on this plane. I felt it happen! My name and Social Security number were the same, but my essence evolved in that moment, thrusting me into a new life.

For at least a year after this dramatic, cosmic intervention, all I did was try to get better by working earnestly on my program. I grieved the loss of my father in my early teens, and the divorce of my mother and stepfather two years later, both losses I'd never let myself feel. My body went through a major purge after ninety days, beginning with a high fever and bronchial inflammation that then raged through my body. I was purging and sobbing at the same time. That was kind of scary.

Some people do this purge more gradually, but I later read about the exact process in a book on Zen healing. The book suggested that, after a purge like this, we will crave some of the things we have let go of. Then, if we don't take them back into our bodies, we will be free from the craving. I had already had a hot fudge sundae and a big steak by that time. Oh well. I did let go of a two-pack-a-day smoking habit after that illness, though.

This kind of radical rearrangement of all of one's molecules is often referred to as a "conversion experience." But like most dominant cultural narratives, conversion stories are most often told through the male experience. The talking Light frequently shows up in conversion stories, but the male-dominant narrative most often adds an element of a punitive self-flagellation. Think Augustine and his hatred of the body, or Paul on the road to Damascus, struck down by a blinding light on his way to kill some more people.

What a great way to waste a miracle!

A supernatural visit pulls you out of utter despair, and the next thing you do is slap on a lot of negatives and rules and restrictions for the new life you've been granted? This was NOT my kind of conversion, thank God.

Women who live in a male-dominated society often become addicted, I believe, after being smashed into male-defined social roles that destroy our volition, our agency, and our power! These roles turn us into female impersonators, or dancers hungry for the male gaze or male approval. Even in recovery, turbaned yogis and 12-Step male "gurus" of all ages abound. The language of 12-Step meetings can be so toxic and illness-based that even the most liberated female spirit can be easily crushed.

In this amazing process of recovery, it is essential for women not to allow the pervasive, male-dominated recovery narrative to clip our wings, just as we have been set free.

The metaphor of the butterfly's conversion from a chrysalis works for me. This transformation is dramatic and not without danger, but it's also an evolution without a lot of imposed rules. For the Monarch butterfly, this conversion/transformation is nothing short of miraculous. It begins as an inner, organic shedding of the outer form of the caterpillar while still inside the chrysalis. Then the caterpillar's head splits open and the skin falls away, while the inside of the chrysalis becomes a kind of goo or slime. The slime miraculously turns into WINGS, and the beautiful butterfly stretches and flies away. What an amazing metaphor! Think Monarch! Think birth! Think LIFE!

My life changed forever, one day at a time.

My transformation happened one night in the depths of hopelessness, when a talking Light entered my room. The Light transformed me in the blink of an eye—but I needed to take a few steps before I could catch up to the new me. Frankly, I can't believe I had resisted hitting bottom for so long.

I never want to go back there. That bottom was my greatest gift. If I ever think I might enjoy a vodka martini with olives in the lobby of the Plaza Hotel, all I have to do is remember that I didn't hit bottom at the Plaza ... not by a long shot. My bottom was a bounce into another dimension, not a crash into a land of shattered bones!

My experience was the first catalyst that began a lifetime of study, teaching, spiritual direction, and counseling people in recovery. This ultimately led me to write my book *The Gateways: The Wisdom of 12-Step Spirituality*, a book about a non-gendered, non-punitive, open-ended, expansive, inter-spiritual, multi-dimensional transformation with ideas and support.

And by the way, this is precisely how the founders of the first 12-Step program described the process of transformation. I'm sticking with them. *"To us, the Realm of Spirit is broad, roomy, all-inclusive, never exclusive or forbidding to those who earnestly seek. It is open, we believe, to all."* — Alcoholics Anonymous, p. 46

Sing your song! Dance your dance! Fly, butterfly, fly!

Mad Dawg Loves Grimm Reaper
by Lynn Forrester

The true definition of "love" is caring about the health, well-being, and happiness of another person to a greater degree than your own. We do that for each other.

After nearly forty years, two marriages two children, and four grandchildren, I am living my love story.

As a twenty-seven-year-old single mom in the early 1980s, I quit the nursing profession and signed on with the Sheriff's Academy of a major metropolitan city. I was only the third female in the Police Department to be hired among the ranks of testosterone in the male-dominated field. After completing the rigorous training and putting up with all the jokes that could be thrown a young woman's way, I began my probation period with the City Police Department. I was determined to complete probation—even if it killed me.

But the police were just as determined to prevent a female from entering their ranks.

I had made it through three Field Training Officers (FTOs) before being assigned to the final training officer, who would either give me a thumbs-up—signaling that I had what it took to be a cop—or a thumbs-down.

Nobody warned me about what I was getting into. The prior FTOs had been hard enough to handle, with their crude remarks, jokes, and a variety of pranks. Then along came a training officer with a wiry frame who was known on the streets as "Mad Dawg."

He was unlike anyone I had ever met.

Mad Dawg had a sense of humor. I never saw him in a bad mood, but I didn't always know when to take him seriously. I couldn't predict what was going to come out of his mouth in the form of conversation or instructions. However, this was the last FTO I had to get through to reach my goal of becoming an officer, so I was intent on figuring him out.

During the last weeks of training, I learned a lot about this guy they called Mad Dawg. He was probably the most honest person I had ever met; faithful to his wife, and in love with his career as a cop. He made police work seem effortless. I had total respect for him as my training officer and wanted him to have the same level of respect for me.

I had no idea why we began receiving so many dead-body calls, but soon found out why....

Over the next four weeks, we handled many calls. Without telling me, Mad Dawg had requested every dead-body call that came in during my training be dispatched to our unit. Eight dead bodies later—with only a few weeks of training left to go—I was dubbed with the nickname "Grimm Reaper."

Finally, my training with Mad Dawg was over. He gave me a thumb's up and I passed, not only with flying colors, but with respect as a cop who could hold her own.

I became the first female on SWAT duty throughout California, but never bragged about it, because of my training with FTO Mad Dawg. He taught me to have respect for myself and to always know the strengths I possessed.

Life was good. I married a fellow cop, and Mad Dawg and his wife were good friends to both my husband and me. Even after Mad Dawg left for another opportunity, our families remained in touch.

Over the years, we both went through many changes. Mad Dawg remarried and had a son, and he and his wife moved to the Pacific Northwest. I retired from the City PD, had a son, and found work as a private investigator while trying to hang on to my marriage and raise two kids.

As the years passed, I lost touch with Mad Dawg and his family. Then one day, while I was researching an old friend, I found out that Mad Dawg was now working for the sheriff's department in Washington State. I called a number, not sure it was the right one, and left a message for him. Mad Dawg called me back an hour or so later.

He seemed to be the same ole' Mad Dawg: happy, crazy, and thrilled to hear from me. We caught up on things. He didn't know I'd been divorced for several years. He was doing fine and living a satisfying life. He said if I ever wanted to visit, he and his family would be glad to have me.

We ended the conversation on a promise to stay in touch—but once again, years passed, and we didn't reconnect.

One day, three years after Mad Dawg and I had spoken, he called again. Something was wrong. He told me his marriage had ended. Nearly forty years had passed, and here we were, both divorced.

His sadness concerned me so I said, "This too shall pass" and told him if he needed someone to talk to, he could call anytime. So began the long phone calls from the Pacific Northwest to Houston—first once a week, and then three-times a week.

There had never been an "attraction" between us, nor had I ever looked at him as a love interest.

My respect was for Mad Dawg as a man who had good character and who loved his family, career, life, and of course, his faith. Yes, I often wished I had someone to care for me the way that he cared for his family, but a love-attraction was just never there.

Fast-forward: We are engaged and will be married in a couple of months. We have spent the last two and a half years getting to know each other outside of our careers and friendship. We have come to understand what it means to be in love with a person for who they are, not for what they can give you. We've learned what it means to say, "I love you."

I now know what real love is; it is not perfect.

But real love is pretty close. Mad Dawg is the same man today he was forty years ago. He is still as crazy as ever and he's a good friend, loyal, honest, and of good character. That's hard to find these days. He drives me crazy, just as he did when we drove together as police officers.

And although we may only have twenty more good years left before God decides differently, we will make the best of those years—laughing, hanging out, enjoying life as it should be, but most importantly, worshiping together. God knew where this would end, and where it would begin, again. I am grateful for God's wisdom.

The true definition of "love" is caring about the health, well-being, and happiness of another person to a greater degree than your own. We do that for each other.

Share a Life? Are You Crazy!

by Joan Chadbourne, EdD

*Thank heavens I had committed to listening to my intuition
and acting on it, or the meeting that changed
my life might never have happened.*

It seemed like a miracle that Chuck and I found each other. Some would probably say we were too old for new love.

Our first meeting, which we scheduled for an hour, lasted five!

When I finally met Chuck in person, I instinctively knew this wasn't going to be a typical meet-and-greet. He arrived early at the coffee shop and welcomed me with a hug that conveyed the warmth of an old friend, not someone I was meeting for the first time.

This is going to be interesting, I thought.

His hug was only the beginning of an extraordinary event. Suddenly, I began to hyperventilate.

This wasn't a subtle struggling for air; it was loud gasps. People sipping lattes noticed. I'd never experienced anything like that before. Five minutes later, my breathing was normal again, but my mind was a complete blank.

Finally, I managed to whisper, "I have no words."

Cancer had taken Chuck's voice twelve years earlier, so he "spoke" using a synthesizer. As he typed, the machine spoke: "Don't worry. I'll take responsibility for the conversation." Even in my state of confusion, the irony of that remark made me smile.

Thank heavens I had committed to listening to my intuition and acting on it, or the meeting that changed my life might never have happened. Each morning prior to meeting Chuck, I had deleted the computer-generated matches sent from my dating service. On the unforgettable day of June 12, 2012, I sat at the computer as usual. However, before I could hit "delete," an authoritative inner voice boomed: *Look further this time.* I listened and found Chuck.

After a flurry of revealing emails, where we shared much about ourselves, we decided to meet at the coffee shop. The night before our initial meeting, we were like a couple of excited teenagers texting 'till the wee hours of the night.

The next day, when we met in person—after I caught my breath—I disclosed that I'd felt rocked to sleep the night before. He smiled at me, his cornflower blue eyes impishly twinkling.

"I fell asleep imagining I was rocking you in my arms," he typed.

Chuck and I were communicating telepathically. We were energetically connected, and I was hooked; but despite our great connection, Chuck had said he would only invest in a relationship with someone who wanted to "share a life." We were in our early seventies, and I had been single for twenty years. That was definitely NOT me!

I'd built a rich and full life living on my own.

I cherished and fiercely protected my independence. Back home, feeling restless, I was compelled to create a five-page, single-spaced report detailing all the reasons we couldn't "share a life." After hitting the "send" button, a sense of calm and relaxation swept over me.

His response? He declined further contact. Chuck wouldn't settle for less than what he wanted. I was crushed, confused, and devastated. *What is going on with me?*

My eyes fell upon my bedside table and saw *Conscious Loving*, a book by Gay and Kathlyn Hendricks. They describe the Upper Limits Problem: We choose how much positive energy we can tolerate and set our limit. When we get close to that threshold, we feel threatened, and our unconscious selves do everything possible to sabotage whatever is bringing us joy—so we can feel safe again.

Could that book be sending me a message? I don't believe in coincidences, but it seemed so relevant. *Had the good feelings been too much?*

Had I sabotaged a delicious possibility?

I needed guidance. For four days and nights, I meditated, prayed, sobbed, and journaled, asking for clarity about what was happening. An insightful friend thought this situation was similar to an early childhood story I'd told her about being *confined* by love. Was that remembrance why I was sabotaging us?

Through this intense questioning process, I discovered the unconscious, core belief that generated my fear and kept me from what I wanted: *The cost of loving and being loved is loss of self. You can have one or the other, not both.*

This unconscious belief had influenced every decision I'd ever made about relationships. Once it was unearthed, my life made sense. It became clear how this conviction had walled me off from any long-term love relationship.

I wailed as I recognized the loneliness and grief this belief had cost me.

It was a major breakthrough. Because our thoughts create our reality, if I changed that belief, I could change my life. By finding the courage to let go of an old idea, my life would be so much more fulfilling. If I tuned in to the loving, energetic soul connection between Chuck and me—and released the fear associated with that old belief—we would have an opportunity for an amazing relationship! With the grace of God, I decided to let go of fear and choose love.

Changing my belief set me free.

That act transformed my life. Although the shift wasn't dependent upon Chuck's response, I fervently hoped that he'd reconsider.

"Yes, I do want to share a life," I wrote to Chuck. "I've changed my mind. I understand this might seem like a suspiciously quick turnaround. Consider it like the seemingly overnight success that actually took years. This quick change required seventy years of life experience. It is real and lasting."

After several days of pondering, Chuck also took a risk. He accepted my invitation to continue exploring. We shared a life, and it was a joyous, expanding, and satisfying one.

We still have a sense of well-being and joy, even though the form of our relationship has shifted. Chuck transitioned into Spirit a year and a half ago. I walk enfolded in the cloak of our love. My consciousness and capacity to love have expanded.

I am never alone. He walks with me. Sometimes, we communicate through mediums. More often, we're discovering numerous ways to connect directly.

Our ever-growing, multidimensional love is a valued gift and comfort. We appreciate and are grateful that the Divine gave us this opportunity. We had to make the courageous decision to nurture our love, and we continue to do so every day.

Third Time Charm

by Denise Alexander Pyle

Letting Go and Letting God

I thought I knew who I was.

As a successful lawyer, politician, and elected city official, I was well known in my community. Now, at age forty—after my second divorce—it was time to search for my "holy grail," my true identity.

Having established a successful law career, I was not afraid to start over in a new direction. It took the form of a new career and a move from my lifelong residency in suburban Detroit to Washington, D.C. Maybe this would be the change I needed to fulfill my longstanding political dreams and ambitions.

My Capitol adventure began with an appointment as a Deputy Assistant Secretary at HUD. The assignment started in July of 1992, in the middle of a presidential election cycle. I knew the job might be short-lived, but the chance to start a new life overshadowed any potential downside. By January 21, 1993—aligned with the outgoing regime—the job was over, and I was left in a new city without a job or any network to help me start over.

Now I was a little fish in a big pond of fish just like me.

And no one was fishing at the moment. I had left Michigan with a lot of fanfare and I didn't want to go back as a failure. Unwilling to admit defeat or return to the life left behind, I sought something different. Twice I had been married to lawyers, and thought that formula would make me happy, but it didn't. Now I realized it hadn't nourished my soul.

Although born and raised Jewish, I had always been a spiritual seeker and had pursued metaphysical knowledge since the age of fourteen. As a young girl, I'd planned on a career as a journalist or a writer. For the first time in my life, I had nowhere to be and the time to pursue who I really was—not what I did for a living.

I had accumulated several books over the years that I'd never quite found the time to read. During the 1980s, after Shirley MacLaine released *Out on a Limb*, it seemed the array of new age reading material exploded. Dan Millman's *Peaceful Warrior* series and Lynn Andrews' *Medicine Woman* were among the inspirational books that would fuel my path to self-discovery, along with older material such as Madame Blavatsky's *Secret Doctrine*.

There were two good metaphysical bookstores in the Metropolitan Washington area, one in Georgetown and one in Alexandria. Although my funds for discretionary spending were limited, I purchased and devoured *The Celestine Prophecy* and more than one hundred other books over the next eight months.

While becoming more immersed in the spiritual community, I formed a master-mind group with a few like-minded women I'd met in the bookstore. During each session, I carefully crafted the vision and outcome to put forth to the Universe for my new life. My expectations were great and I thought I could control my destiny.

My personal life was another matter.

My judgment in relationships was proving untrustworthy. A few casual relationships occupied my time, but the prospect of remarriage was not in my direct line of vision. I did, however, acquire a well-written affirmation list containing all the attributes for the perfect soul mate. The list had become part of my daily prayer ritual. The rest was supposed to be up to God, but I still had a preconceived image of what this perfect person would look like, once I was ready to allow him into my life. Since I was in Washington D.C., he was probably a handsome Washington lawyer or power broker, right?

Wrong. The Universe had something different in store for me.

By Fall 1993, I was finally getting a few clients, including some through my home base in Michigan. My niece in Colorado, who was turning thirty, came for a visit. We took a road trip together back to the Detroit area, to see family and finish some work.

She was into the country dancing craze, and I went along to watch. On Saturday October 2nd, we went to dinner and then to a country bar in Pontiac, Michigan called Diamonds and Spurs. My pregnant girlfriend joined us, but by 10:30 p.m., she was ready to go home. My niece hadn't found anyone she really wanted to dance with, so she was fine with leaving, too. However, after dropping off my friend, she suggested we try another county bar nearby. I agreed to go for "just a little while."

It was almost midnight when we walked into Dominick's. My life has never been the same since!

We stood at a high-top table near the bar and watched the scene. The crowd was beginning to thin out when a man approached and asked me to dance. He wore a black cowboy hat and a New Orleans T-shirt. He definitely didn't look like *my* type, whatever that was, and I didn't really know the steps to the dances. I responded, "Why don't you dance with my niece? She is two-stepping across the country."

So, he did, and he was actually a good dancer. After a few dances, they returned to my table and we began a conversation. He said his name was Steve. He was easy to talk to and personable. A song came on that he liked and again, he asked me to dance—and again, I pawned him off on my niece, still insecure about my own dance skills. She was only too happy to have a good dance partner. After they danced a few dances, he came back again to talk to me. A non-country song called The Hustle played. Now it was my turn on the dance floor.

When this cowboy realized I loved to dance and could move, he started to teach me the steps to the country dances. We danced a little while before my niece, perturbed that I had taken her dance partner, said it was late and time to leave.

Steve asked if I'd be interested in continuing the dance lesson the following Sunday night back at Diamonds and Spurs. We agreed to meet, but not as a date, because I was heading back to Washington on Tuesday.

While I normally pride myself on being prompt, I showed up at the bar an hour late. My niece had planned to go with me, but when she was nowhere to be found, I finally left by myself and headed for Pontiac. Steve was already on the dance floor, so I went to the bar and ordered a soft drink. He noticed me after the song ended and headed straight to me.

Before he said anything, I found myself babbling an apology for being late. He responded that he had been about to leave when I didn't show at the designated time. He generally did not go out on a Sunday night because he had to get up for work very early, but on this night, something kept telling him to wait.

We didn't do much dancing. Instead, we found ourselves deeply engrossed in conversation as we began learning about each other. He was a Quaker farm boy from Marion, Indiana who worked as a mid-level, salaried manager and trouble-shooter, manufacturing cars for General Motors. He had been divorced for several years and said he didn't like lawyers or politicians. I laughed and agreed with him, even as I admitted to being both.

A question he'd asked in an earlier conversation intrigued me the most. "Did you ever wonder if, when a fish is caught and pulled out of the water into the bright sunshine, to face the fisherman taking him off the hook before throwing him back into the water, the fish goes back to the other fish and describes it as a beautiful, near-death-experience of being immersed in bright light and looking into the face of God? The fish didn't know it at the time, but on another day, he might have ended up on a dinner plate." He followed with, "Are we just the fish in some other sea?" Still waters ran very deep in this man.

When the bar closed, we moved to another one until it, too, closed. I declined his invitation to go back to his house to continue our conversation, because we both had to be at work in just a few hours. We politely exchanged numbers. I actually wrote his number on the back of one of my own business cards.

He asked if we could see each other or talk again before I left, but I was booked well into the following evening with meetings. Also, I was getting back into my "real" world and didn't see any real point. To this quasi-New Age Jewish girl, Steve appeared to be an All-American, gentile country-bumpkin.

I hadn't seen change coming like a freight train.

Back at home Tuesday night, two messages from Steve were on my answering machine. The first one was benign, but I took notice of the second message. This man had put himself "out there" and professed his feelings for me.

Although I was still unsure of my feelings, he deserved a call back right away. But the card with his number was gone! Apparently, I had accidently given it to someone the previous day. Steve's number was unlisted, so he was going to have to wait.

The next morning, I called General Motors and got his work number from employee information and explained to him why I hadn't called earlier. We got to know each other during phone conversations over the next several nights.

By Saturday morning, our phone bills were mounting. We agreed that we needed to spend real time together and confirm our connection. This man—who claimed he never drove across town to pick up a date, because there were a million women in between—proceeded to drive to Washington D.C. with his dog to find out the answer to his questions about me.

When I saw him again, I still wasn't sure I hadn't invited some psycho person into my home.

But Steve continued to surprise me all weekend. I had always considered myself the spiritual sparkler for my friends but being with Steve was like being with Socrates from the *Way of the Peaceful Warrior*. He challenged me to throw away my preconceived notions. I knew there would be more spiritual adventures ahead.

We made plans to reconnect in Michigan two weeks later—but it was the weekend in between that would seal our fate. It was then I truly let go and allowed God to change my life.

I was at the Siddha Yoga Meditation Center in the Catskill Mountains of New York with three relatively new female acquaintances, looking for some kind of sign to validate my connection with Steve. I figured this was the place to find it. Rising early that Saturday morning to attend the dawn service, I hoped the Gurumayi, their spiritual leader, would say something profound to me while receiving her blessings. But it didn't happen.

Disappointed and alone, I went to my room to change and found something surprising on my bed: a sheet cake that said, "Happy Eternal Life." Where did the cake come from and what did it mean? I left to get one of my companions, but when we returned a few minutes later, the cake was gone! Now, where did it go?

Then it hit me. This was the message I was seeking. Let go and let God, and I will have a "happy eternal life."

The next weekend, I returned to Michigan to spend more time with Steve. My plan was to stay until Monday morning, but the weekend got extended until Wednesday. Why? Because Steve and I got married on Tuesday, October 26, 1993.

My soul mate affirmation list became part of our vows.

By getting out of my own way and allowing God to work through me, I was transformed, and my life was forever changed. I returned to Michigan and learned that, even without my titles, I was still the same worthy person. However, a very different lawyer built a successful family law practice founded in love and a passion for justice in place of ego.

And yes, Steve truly does walk the walk. My journey with him has been the best change of all.

Gifts Within a Sacred Wound
by Glenda-Ray Riviere

Be-Loved I AM, Be-Loved YOU Are, Be-Loved WE Are.

As a young child, I experienced being neither seen nor heard. I remember hiding behind the curtain, wondering what might happen if I dared to express my feelings, thoughts, or emotions freely. Silence found me instead. But all of these unexpressed emotions and feelings had to go somewhere, and somewhere turned out to be the bathtub.

I was a young adult who was beginning to identify who I was or was not in this world. While sitting in the tub washing my locks, something appeared out of nowhere in my hand. Could this be? Was that dark clump my *hair?*

More appeared. No! This was not happening. It must be a nightmare! When I stepped out of the tub with my hand full of dark masses of hair, I looked into the mirror and saw someone different. My eyebrows should have been un-plucked and full—and now they were gone! Thin lines appeared above the eyes that looked back at me.

Painfully fast, painfully slow, all of my hair fell out.

Yes, all fell out from within, including all those unexpressed thoughts, feelings, and emotions. Who was I now? Who would ever want me? My dear mother offered to help by suggesting I use makeup to draw on a face.

Oh, how she tried, in her matter-of-factness, to lighten things up— or was it to darken them? My loving sister with her warm, gentle hand brought me to a salon to be fitted with a scratchy wig to cover up my head, so I could be seen in public. Her heart so desired to make things better. I tried to smile and pretend all was fine, again.

This was the hiding or pushing away of words I longed to scream. Was it me, or my world? "Yes! Make the world stop!" I cried out to my mother of birth. "Stay home with me. No more work. No more school."

"Oh, my," Mother replied while making her bed. "Vanity is a funny thing, isn't it, dear?"

Time passed while I pretended to cope.

Why couldn't everything just STOP? The following years saw me just going through the motions. One day, I found myself in the hospital, barely able to breathe; full-blown pneumonia was ravaging my lungs, leaving me with only 20 percent capacity to breathe the breath of life.

The doctor said, in a matter-of-fact way, "We will do the best we can." My parents stood at the foot of the bed, glancing at their watches, worried about their parking meter running out of time.

One night, I heard a voice. Was it mine or another's?

"Weed your garden. It is time to weed your garden!"

I remember being poked and prodded, prodded and poked, and screaming at someone. Words were spoken that were NOT my truth. NO! How dare you tell them how I feel? You have NO idea.

My memory of the journey within those four hospital walls was vivid. Looking out a window at a tree, in awe of a bird eating a worm, feeling deeply moved by the experience—as if I was the bird and the bird was me. I remembered a song my dear brother used to sing to me as a young child.

♫ *"Brenda-bird up high in banana tree, Brenda bird won't you sing along with me? Won't you fly away in the sky away?"*

I felt a raw vulnerability—half naked, partly covered, partly not.

Someone was behind me. Turning around, I noticed my sister sitting in a chair. Her eyes bugged out when she saw what was standing at the window: me. That same loving sister who had held my hand and guided me to the salon to cover up my head with that scratchy thing was shocked by my appearance.

"Is *that* my sister?" she asked quietly, and then stood with her mouth open.

I persistently demanded to go home, without having any perspective about how I really felt inside. A perspective compared to what? Compared to the bird in that tree? My memories were of feeling part here, part not, and being asked to weed my garden, and being in my physical shelter instead of the world out there.

Weeks later—or was it a lifetime—the doctor reluctantly discharged me from the hospital.

During this physical, mental, and emotional roller coaster ride, I started to finally express what had been buried deep within me. A rush of gratitude spontaneously found me, and I began creating a gratitude chain that grew and grew. It wrapped itself around every sacred chamber of my home-heart. The message on each link was written in a moment of feeling deep gratitude for some simple thing: being able to pour myself a glass of water, seeing the sun shine through the window, hearing a child laughing in the distance.

My life evolved before my eyes.

I became aware that my perception of everyday experiences had somehow changed. A spider in a web touched my heart. Was I the spider and the web, delicate and strong at the same time?

The setting for my new life was the kitchen, where I learned to prepare nutrition for which my body longed. Along with new recipes, I found new ways of nourishing and experiencing and expressing. I carried a journal wherever I traveled, even if it was just a walk in nature, and recorded the reflections and revelations that sprang forth out of nowhere and everywhere. My sacred story wrote itself from the gifts within the wound.

The medicine of now is what I bring forth to the world. My journey has been one of realizing, remembering, and acknowledging that the only person who can truly see me, acknowledge me, hear me, love me, and accept me is my-self.

Through these awakening experiences, and the integration of these lessons through self-realization, I commanded the Universe to show me another way of healing and empowerment. The Universe responded by presenting me with many different forms of healing such as Reiki, Theta Healing, Re-Connective Healing, and meditation. By exploring the various healing modalities that resonated with me, I forged deeper into my journey of Self-remembrance. I was finding my-self and re-creating my-self, again and again, by speaking my truth and establishing boundaries.

Anything that might have interfered with love and acceptance of myself and my sacred experiences fell away. I had come home to my Heart; it had always been there, ready to be received, remembered, and embraced fully. This infinite, never-ending journey of Self-love, growth, and ever-expanding consciousness happened spontaneously once I commanded the Universe to show me another way.

Years passed.

One day, I woke up and became aware through a heart-knowing that my purpose here on this Earth was to be an energy healer. My job was to show people that there is, indeed, another way to transform and integrate lessons in the moment so that energy does not get trapped in the body and manifest as physical illness.

The body, heart, and soul speak to us each moment—if we dare to listen and heed their messages. Perpetual "pain" is just a crying to be acknowledged. It asks to receive the messages, to integrate the lessons, and take the action or non-action. We strive to speak our truth, to be seen and heard, to be received, embraced, and held in a sacred space of compassion for ourselves.

This journey of peeling back the layers and shedding the mask, to reveal the tenderness of the gifts within, is now the unique, authentic medicine I share with others. I had transformed and integrated it into the wholeness of my being: to be in Service to the Love-That-I-Am, exactly as I AM, through my sacred journey, with no beginning and no ending. My gift is self-realization, remembrance, transformation, and empowerment.

As the sacred story wrote itself so that I could share my truth, my relationships to significant others in my life also transformed, right before my eyes. They became a reflection of the harmony within me. There is no "other." The other is me.

Today, my relationship with my mother is an entirely different reality.

She now sees her daughter through different eyes. She acknowledges me and loves me in a way I had never experienced as a child. My mother now mirrors the harmony of my relationship to the mother/child within me, as I have allowed the mother within to nurture me, see me, love me, and embrace me.

I can go deeper with this experience by holding space and nurturing the mother/child within, and by having compassion for myself and all of my experiences. No longer pointing fingers at others has created a deep, sacred space for healing, which also allows me to be able to hold space for others. By not giving away my power to my mother—which had been a reflection of the disharmony of the mother/child relationship within me—I have more love and compassion. The realization and awareness of that lesson not only assisted in my healing, but also gave me the ability to hold sacred space for my mother in her transformation.

By seeing her already loved, loveable, caring, compassionate, and valuing her self-worth, my experience of my mother transformed. When we are empowered in the awareness that everything we experience comes from within us, healing happens spontaneously. We are neither going outside of ourselves to find the answers nor blaming others.

Rather, I acknowledged and asked my heart, "What would love choose right now? What would be a loving solution?" Similarly, by asking the question, "If I knew the lesson in this experience, what would I know it to be?" I was shown the answer.

One day, I was drawn to the sound of soothing music in a metaphysical bookstore. I walked over to the counter and asked my heart to guide me to the music that was healing me.

The picture on the music CD's cover sparked an aversion in me, but I became curious. Hmmm. Maybe the aversion is really the medicine. The music began playing in my home-heart. Dancing and crying to the sacred sound, I spontaneously chanted, "Beloved I Am." The sound came out of nowhere—or was it my heart singing through me, to me?

Healing for One is Healing for All.

Once again, I found myself in the bathtub, chanting over and over again. Stepping out of the tub and looking into the mirror, the reflection now showed that healing waters had cleansed the core of my being. Tears I did not know existed sprang forth, cellular, ancient, and ancestral—tears shed over my many lifetimes.

Through this journey of uncovering the layers to reveal the gifts within the sacred wound—and commanding to be shown another way—it was revealed to me that I am the master creator of my reality. I have within me everything necessary to transform, empower my journey, and create the life of my heart's desire.

I am grateful for my transformational experiences and the healing I can integrate and embody through Self-realization. This is my medicine, for me and for the consciousness of our planet.

May we all remember why we came here: to remember that we are love, and that love IS the way through Home to the Heart. May we all receive and integrate messages from our sacred wounds to reveal the gifts within them, to heal ourselves and the planet.

May we all live *from* the Sacred Heart, *through* the Sacred Heart, and *as* the Sacred Heart. With every thought, word, and deed may we assist humanity in raising the consciousness of the planet through Self-realization—the healing and transformation of our unique soul's journey.

Final Thoughts

As many stories in this section suggested, the pursuit of love and relationships can be a matter of focus, perception, and looking in the mirror. According to research[1], that crazy little thing called love has been called a socially acceptable "divine madness" for good reason, as seen in films[2] and books. History is filled with dramatic displays of love: the Taj Mahal was built by an emperor grieving his wife.[3] According to research in *Psychology Today*[4], "The most important thing to feel is that you are loved. Life without love is barely tolerable."

Could it be that, when we become the right person, we meet the right person—often when we least expect it, in the strangest of places, and seldom when we are actively looking?

As many of the stories in this section portrayed, self-love is the key to maintaining successful relationships, even with ourselves. Does love show up, or is it always there, shrouded by the fog of self-doubt and emotional pain? Once the fog lifts, true love may be revealed. Love is timely and timeless, as shown by Joan Chadbourne, who never wanted to fall in love again ("Are You Crazy?") or like a Grimm Reaper falling in love with a Mad Dawg.

This crazy little thing called love can turn our world upside down, just as issues with our health can, as seen in the next section: *Health and Well-Being: I'll Stand by You.*

PART 2

HEALTH AND WELL-BEING
I'll Stand by You

Never fear the unknown
For it has answers for you
That you may not have considered

Dreaming Healing, Again!
by Kathleen O'Keefe-Kanavos

*By combining the intuitive aspects of healing with modern
medicine, I had a prescription for healing that was
greater than the sum of its individual parts.*

nable to sit still, I wait at this world-renowned hospital for my
mammogram to be read in front of me. I'm scared out of my
mind but not sure why. The moment reminds me of a dream
I had five years earlier, right before the pathology report diagnosing my
breast cancer.

Being on the List

*A young secretary in a hospital waiting room holds a clipboard in her hand
and says, "You're on the list. The doctors are going to call you. You have let
this go on for far too long, and now it has gotten into everything." Then she
disappears.[1]*

Although I'd had a normal mammogram, blood test, and physical exam a
few weeks before, the dream had guided me to self-advocate for a second
set of tests, and those eventually found cancer the conventional tests had
missed.

A few weeks after the dream and lumpectomy, the doctors called to tell me the tumor that nobody had seen on the mammograms was more massive than they'd initially thought. Rather than early, Stage One breast cancer, it was Stage Two, and they'd also found it in a lymph node. The pathology report had validated my dream.

My dream had been a warning that the cancer was much worse than expected. Should I have been stronger at self-advocating that first time, five years earlier? And how could I have done so?

Now its five years later, almost to the day, and my life is imitating my dreams again—or is it the other way around?

I'm cold and clammy. These are the symptoms of a classic anxiety attack. What is wrong?

Perhaps the answer is evident to me because I've been hearing unintelligible whispering in the background of my mind all day.

Why the hell am I so frightened?

A voice distracts me from my mental babble. "The doctor is ready to see you, Ms. Kanavos." The nurse is pointing to a list of names on a clipboard.

"Congratulations!" the seated doctor says.

My eyes strain to adjust in the dark cubbyhole of an office. Back-lit walls display multiple mammography photos with my name printed in bold, black letters at the bottom. No doubt about it, these pictures are mine.

"Your mammogram is healthy," the doctor announces.

An inner-voice counters with, ***Don't believe it!*** *Look, right here and here. Oh shit, where did you come from? Here we go again!*

As I pull my gown closer around my trembling body, a hooded monk-guide from my previous dreams is standing beside me. My breasts are under attack … again.

"Are you sure?" I ask the radiologist. "What about over here?" My finger points as if it's being led by an invisible hand.

The doctor faces me, looks surprised, and then motions to the other mammogram and replies, "That's not the breast that had cancer. You are healthy." And as if to send the message home (or dismiss me), he shakes my hand and says, "Get dressed." The monk-guide is gone.

"Yeah, okay. Thanks. Bye." *Perhaps the voice and the monk were just my imagination.*

My husband asks what is wrong. "Nothing. The doctor said I'm healthy."

He's confused because of my positive words juxtaposed with my negative body language. He knows I should be doing cartwheels of joy up and down the hallway from this good news. *Happiness* should be written all over my face. But it isn't. And I don't want to alarm him with "my monks, voices, and gut-instincts" when things seem to be going so well.

"But I still want to get an MRI. I'll ask Dr. Harold to make an appointment for me now."

Dr. Harold is already waiting for me. "Dr. Goopka called and said you were on your way down here, Kathy." *That's odd. How did he know?*

"We both think you're suffering from anxiety. Go home. You're healthy."

Later that evening, while lying in the bathtub, I pour water over my head while poring over the day's events. Which to believe … my voices and instincts, or my mammograms? My dreams and intuitions had saved my life once before when my cancer diagnosis was missed. Are they trying to rescue me again?

What a frightening thought! But history might be repeating itself. I want so badly to believe the doctors and tell my voices to leave me alone. But I don't think I can—or should. I don't think I dare.

I'll sleep on the information before deciding which to believe: the healthy medical results or my celestial voices.

A dream that night makes my decision for me.

The Scary Medical Monk Clowns Dream
Two monk-guides in brown, hooded cassocks pull me from my previous dream into a brightly lit, white hospital room where a third female robed guide holds up my mammograms in one hand and points to them with the other. My name, in bold block letters, shows they are mine. It is unusual that she wears a white medical coat with matching white clogs over her rope belted robe rather than just the customary hooded cassock and leather sandals. Reluctantly, I inch closer and peer at the film, but I see nothing. She shoves one plate closer, points to it again, and grimaces like a terrifying circus clown. Then, POOF! She instantly transforms into one. She wears a colorful clown suit, a curly red wig, and huge shoes sporting big red balls on the toes and shrieks with laughter while rocking back and forth. "Wake up, wake up!" I yell. "This is a nightmare!"[2]

No dream dictionary is necessary to decipher this nightmare. I've GOT IT!

Now I believe my voices and precognitive dreams over my mammography film—but how do I win over the doctors? I'll know tomorrow when I show up at Dr. Harrold's office without an appointment. I'll be armed with my puny war chest of dreams while he'll have a big medical bag full of indisputable evidence. How weird is this? Someone wake me up! Oh yeah, I AM awake, and my dreams are bleeding into my waking world.

I know I need that MRI.

"Kathy, all of your mammograms are healthy, as are your blood tests and physical exams," Dr. Harold says at my appointment. This moment is *déjà vu!* Have I been transported back in time to four-and-a-half years earlier, when Dr. Wagner told me the same thing? "It's not hospital policy to order MRIs without a good reason. They can give you false positives."

"I don't trust mammograms, and with good reason," I counter. "I've had negative mammograms before that should have been positive. Please order the MRI, too."

His intense blue eyes study me. "Okay, tell my secretary to make an appointment. I'll see you in a year."

"Sorry," the secretary says. "Nothing's available, but I'll call you when something is."

One month later, I am back in the doctor's office.

The secretary has called and said she couldn't find an open appointment to get me an MRI this year. Now, since more than thirty days have passed, I'll need another appointment and the doctor will have to order it again. So here I am again … frustrated.

How can I convince the medical community about the importance of this test? It's not only because of my dream. If mammography did not find my cancer the first time, shouldn't they be using a different test to watch for recurrence? Doctors need to change the protocol they use for detecting recurrence.

I know an explanation of "I had this scary guided-doctor-clown dream" won't get me the additional test I need. In fact, describing my dream might get me committed to a padded cell for life—which, if I don't get the MRI soon, might not be very long! However, if I want a change in how patients are diagnosed for cancer, I must be the change I wish to see—starting right now.

"Okay. Go out and have my secretary make the appointment for you."

"That doesn't work," I reply. "Please, you go tell her again."

He tells her—and again, it doesn't work. "We didn't make the last appointment," she says after the doctor has left.

"Well, who did? The results and request must be in my file."

"Try Dr. Barkley's office on the ninth floor."

Peter and I head for the elevator. Nine minutes and nine floors later, I hear the same answer from Dr. Barkley's secretary, who sends us to the seventh floor, where I get a similar response. A few more minutes in the elevator, and I'm back where I started, two floors below ground level in nuclear medicine.

But now, I'm not in a good mood!

"I think this is called a run-around," I hiss at Dr. Harold's secretary. "I'm done. Make the appointment for me right now, because I'm not … repeat NOT … leaving this office until you do. You can get security on the phone and ask them to drag me out of here by my heels. On my way out, I'll be calling Channel 2 News. I want that MRI appointment NOW!"

My MRI appointment is scheduled.

They say, "Those who don't learn from history are doomed to repeat it." Experience has taught me that I must self-advocate, in the strongest terms possible, when I find I am not being taken seriously. I know I wouldn't be having "guided dreams" if I were not meant to live.

IF the results of this MRI are what I think they will be, this is way beyond *déjà vu*, history, and synchronicity. This is a direct, divine, life-saving intervention from the other side.

The next morning, after the exam, my doctor gives me the news. "Kathy, we're all in a state of shock over your MRI results. We've already held a meeting with the department heads."

My doctor watches my eyes to see if the statement registers. It does! Bad news! The voices and doctor-dream-clowns were not just my imagination. "According to the MRI, you have a five centimeter tumor in your left breast—not the right breast, where you had your original cancer."

My biopsy results acknowledge my "voices" and validate my precognitive dreams. They have saved my life a second time. The large mass in my breast—which was missed by years of mammograms, blood tests, and physical examinations—is cancer… again … only this time, it is bigger and far more dangerous. However, awareness is the beginning of change. I now have the attention of the medical community. I can change the direction of my health.

Thank God for my dreams, determination, and self-advocacy.

The first time I approached a doctor after a precognitive warning dream, five years earlier, he might have responded like this: "I don't feel anything, and you had a normal mammogram, but let's take a look with the office's ultrasound machine. If we still don't see anything, I'll set up an appointment for an MRI. If something shows up on the MRI, we can do a needle biopsy and consult an oncologist." Yeah, that's how it would happen in a perfect world. Now, back to the real world.

I have learned three things from this second dream-experience:
1. I have to yell and scream if my voice is not respected or heard by those treating my health.
2. When an inner voice communicates, I'd better LISTEN, because
3. There are no norms. There is only me.

I am grateful to my inner guidance for alerting me to a life-threatening illness and to my doctors for treating me, once they confirmed the health issue by conventional means. By combining the intuitive aspects of healing with modern medicine, I now possess a prescription for healing that is greater than the sum of its individual parts.

Honestly, I'm too busy to die. I have a book to write from journals kept during this second cancer treatment. There won't be time to fit in death. Death will have to wait, again.

My lifeline is divided into two parts: BC (Before Cancer) and AD (After Diagnosis). The AD time of my life has taught me that I am stronger than I ever imagined, and that self-advocating is an essential part of life.

As I write this story, I have been cancer-free a second time for fifteen years. Breast cancer, even a recurrence, is not a death sentence. And I'm living proof that dreams do come true—and they can save lives. Dreams are my sacred doorways to Divine Messages.

Now My Family Genes Fit into My Denim Jeans!

by Kristi Tornabene

Searching my family genetic history helped me discover where my health issues began, but it was up to me to make them end.

Kristi, you're getting fat!

My husband's mantra went on long enough to make me look twice in the mirror and ask myself some big questions about my shape and my eating habits. I loved to eat out. At age forty-three, I didn't notice anything terribly wrong with how my butt looked in my jeans. Yet, I was troubled by digestive issues. *Maybe I should consider making some lifestyle changes.*

During this time, my father's health was failing. Around the age of seventy, he had begun losing mobility. At seventy-six, he'd entered a nursing home after it became too difficult for my mother and me to care for him. The nursing home had challenges, and Dad often languished in bed, waiting more than an hour for someone to help him to the bathroom. When he didn't get out of bed one day, he was sent to the hospital and diagnosed with pneumonia and sepsis. That was the last time I saw my father alive. He died that night. He was seventy-nine years old.

My mom, although still active, had gained fifty pounds as she aged. Like me, Mom was always hungry. Then one day, she wasn't hungry anymore. She stopped eating. About a month later, I held her hand as she took her last breath. My mother's side of the family has a history of Type 2, adult-onset diabetes. My mother's death certificate listed "diabetes mellitus" as the cause of death.

After my parents' deaths, I took a long, hard look at my body, my health, and my aches and pains.

How much of what I was feeling was because of my lifestyle, and how much was genetics? What permanent changes could I make to override my inherited genes? Was that even possible?

I decided to investigate what "healthy" meant for my digestive system. My awareness of food-related issues had begun when I'd worked part-time in a grocery store pharmacy, which allowed access to prepackaged foods in the deli department. Prepackaged foods were quick to eradicate my hunger but made me gain weight.

As I began to enter menopause, I changed jobs. Now I sat all day at a desk in an insurance agency. I was no longer moving around, filling prescriptions, and unloading merchandise to the shelves. My body started complaining. Hours of sitting made my hip pain worse, and my lack of movement caused constipation.

I contemplated my family's longevity. If I was this inactive now, how would I be able to keep moving until age ninety? I was already experiencing more pain. Was it from aging? I had to find out. And I had to figure out how to feel full and to keep my hip strong and pain-free and my colon moving. A good diet seemed the logical place to start.

My diet merry-go-round began.

A high protein, good fat diet didn't work. All the protein and fat seemed to collect around my butt. Constipation was my new constant companion, and my husband complained about my belly fat—which, by the way, seemed to resemble the belly of my paternal grandfather. My new job was stressful, which made me voraciously hungry. Then I'd become fearful because I didn't have a deli handy for quick food. Eating stopped the anxiety, but it packed on the pounds.

I had fallen into a vicious hunger cycle. What could I do?

I did what any stressed and out-of-control, peri-menopausal or menopausal woman would do: I self-prescribed high doses of chocolate candy bars. Sugaring up my body pushed my weight higher, and every sugar high led to a sugar crash, and then more hunger.

Next, I tried a diet of protein, vegetables, and a small amount of fat. The new diet made me feel better, and more importantly, the hunger that seemed to have control over my body began fading. These foods helped me feel satiated for about four hours before I needed another meal or snack.

However, having any energy seemed to be a thing of the past. A friend suggested I try choosing food according to what was good for my blood type. On this diet, the increase in my energy was gratifying. Energy had become more important to me than losing weight—although my husband still badgered me.

For the most part, the constipation—which had moved into my life as my new best friend—had been evicted. My intestines still had good days and bad days; my digestion would improve, increase to great, and then screech to a halt. My body had to adapt to my new way of eating. I learned to adjust my diet to stabilize my digestion, to be in-the-moment and choose my food accordingly.

My health and well-being became my passion and my purpose in life.

Looking at my family's genetic history helped me discover where my health issues began, but it was up to me to bring those issues to an end. I knew I didn't need to live with the same pain, digestive issues, and weight gain that my parents and grandparents had suffered, and I didn't have to feel the endless, nagging hunger that had plagued my mother. Comparing my issues with their issues armed me with the knowledge I needed. I have been able to move beyond suffering and into a pain-free future. Remaining strong in my later years of life is important to me.

Once I discovered that most of my health challenges stemmed from eating inflammatory foods, it became my mission to make the changes necessary to resolve those issues and live my best life. I've had to continuously modify my diet, particularly watching how much protein I eat, because my digestive system doesn't always deal well with protein. That was just the first step on this ever-changing journey to excellent, pain-free health.

Choosing healthy foods that I enjoy is at the center of my daily quest to answer the question, "What am I going to eat today?"

For some people, the food challenge is easy: Change this, drink or eat that, and they are done and feeling great. But it's never going to be that simple for me. I've learned I must pay close attention to how my body feels. I'm diligent in checking in with my body and feed it what it needs. After all, it's the only body I have!

Before becoming aware of healthy foods, I had always gravitated toward the easiest and quickest meals. Could I find quick foods that tasted good and also worked for me? That was my goal—and in time, I found them!

This process has given me the ability to figure out exactly what my body needs when I experience certain tell-tale signs, which now point me in the right direction— instead of to the candy bars. My days of the latest fad diet ended once I discovered how to listen to my body and let it tell me how to heal. I have vowed never to go back to eating the way I used to.

Change can mean a more productive and fun life.

Now, at the age of sixty-five, I finally know it takes time for the nutrients from food to get into my cells. Overeating will not get them there sooner. I've learned to be patient with myself and to find something else to do to take my mind off food, so I won't stress over hunger or food choices. My focus has shifted from eating to healing.

People will change when change is necessary. Hip pain and poor digestion got my wellness train rolling and healing has kept me on track. I wish I could snap my fingers, and everything would be right. I wish a magic pill could "fix" me, or I could do just one thing to be healthy—but that's not how it works.

Change is inevitable, but suffering through change is not necessary. Change IS good. I feel twenty years younger than when my journey began, and I can happily report that I am pain-free. My husband has stopped nagging me about my weight. In fact, at the age of eighty-three, he has now embarked on his own journey to wellness.

Examining my physical issues and changing the foods I eat became my ticket to wellness. I'm happy I bought that ticket. My life is so much different, now that I can fit my family genes into my denim jeans.

Fortitude Wins the Battle

by Connie Bramer

I learned that fortitude is a raw necessity when you are facing tough times and that it comes from a deep place within.

Albert Einstein coined the phrase, "Insanity is doing the same thing over and over again and expecting different results." By that definition, we all live in a state of insanity. We get up, get our kids ready and off to school, drive to work, cook dinner, wrangle the kids into bed, and then we do it all over again, waiting for things to get better. If that's not the definition of insanity, it's close.

I was there once—and then everything changed. All of a sudden, it was like the quarter in a coin toss landed on its side and stayed there for months. This coin toss forced a change in the cycle of insanity—my insanity.

When you're told that you have cancer, everything you think about yourself and your life changes. What is this foreign invader rampaging through my body like an army of vicious red ants? As a single working mom, what will happen to my kids if I don't win this battle? And what man will ever want to share a life with me after this crisis? These were the questions that haunted me.

The most apparent and outward change was to my body.

In a strange way, we all take our bodies for granted, believing that they will "hold up" through life's many challenges. But the sight of my body without breasts shocked me and wounded me to the core.

I was mystified that something entirely outside of my control could take a part of my body from me. During chemotherapy, weight fell off me as if I were a melting popsicle in the heat of summer. The "ideal weight" I had once strived for was now higher on the scale. I didn't recognize myself anymore.

I remember going shopping for new jeans with one of my friends from college, because nothing fit me anymore. I had always worn a size 6 or 8. Now, those sizes hung off me. In a size 8, I looked like I was wearing a potato sack in a children's race.

I was astonished when cancer put me into the coveted size 2.

Size 2 is the template for skinny girls. I had never been able to get there on my own, but with cancer's help, I became skinny! Was that a bright side to this mess? It didn't really make the disease worth it, but it seemed like a plus for a while.

At a school function, one of those perfect, size-2 skinny-moms saw me and exclaimed, "You look AMAZING! What have you been doing?"

My response could have been, "I've been spending three hours a day at the gym, and I only eat egg whites and drink tea now." That's what she probably did.

Instead, I said, "Oh, just a little chemotherapy every other week for the last four months."

I couldn't help myself. I was still snarky. Needless to say, she looked around for the nearest "jaws of life" to extricate her perfect size-8 foot from her mouth. I felt a little bad, but … not really.

Cancer was chipping away at me, but on the inside, I was still me.

Journaling became my soul's therapy.

Keeping my sense of humor and writing about the crazy things that happened to me was my way of mentally coping with all of it. I found humor in every part of the journey: the up sides, and even the down sides of cancer. I wrote about the good, the bad, and especially the ugly. Writing became my release and gave me a sense of control during the chaos of cancer. I still had a mind and a mouth. I used both to give a voice to my cancer journey.

But I was also still a mom with two young kids who needed me. I was not about to fail them—and I wouldn't allow them to see my body failing. I strategically scheduled my chemotherapy so I would be ill when they were with their dad. I hid my pain from them.

They didn't need to witness me praying to the porcelain goddess.

Parenting was the one area of my life where I refused to change. Other aspects of my life were undergoing radical revision, but not this one. Of course, the kids could see that I was bald and thinner than before—but I never allowed my role as a parent to waver. I felt it was imperative to show up for all school functions and soccer games. I might have been tired and worn out, but that was not going to make me miss anything. I would be there for my kids—even if it killed me.

The most significant change came in the way I thought about myself.

I was recently divorced—by my choice. I usually only run when I'm being chased, and there are certain tracks I refuse to run on—including the path that leads to the insane asylum. I knew that, if I were still married, he would have had to be there for me through the hellish mess of cancer. He would have had to accept me for who I was. After all, we had said the whole "in sickness and in health, until death do us part" bit.

But things were different now. I was on my own.

I was running on an altogether different path—because I was single again. In my twenties, being unattached had seemed fun and exciting. Fast-forward to my forties, and the joy of being alone was different. I felt like a newly ousted contestant on the TV show *Survivor* must have felt when their flame was snuffed.

It is always hard being single. It was even harder being a single, disfigured cancer survivor. Who would want me now? I'm not going to lie; this was a hard pill to swallow. And trust me, I had become accustomed to swallowing plenty of pills on my way back to wellness. Yet in the throes of all this, I only allowed myself five-minute meltdowns.

Anyone on the outside looking in probably thought I melted down once every hour. Actually, I only allowed myself mini meltdowns once a week. I don't enjoy crying. To me, it feels like a useless waste of energy, even if it does release the troublesome *agita* of life.

It all hit me in the dark of night, as I lay alone in bed.

My life had turned upside down. When would it turn upside right again?

Change is formidable, but sometimes it helps us view things in a different light. I stopped taking excellent health for granted. I realized the truth in the statement, "Without your health, you have nothing." Sometimes I pictured myself as a ship on its side—like the Titanic before it reached the breaking point and sank. My family, my friends, and my doctors served as the anchors to keep me upright and floating. Had it not been for them, I certainly would have sunk deep into the abyss.

After all of the chemotherapy and the plethora of surgeries required to right my body back to some semblance of healthy womanhood, I sadly let go of my size 2 jeans. Gradually, I got back to looking like me. It was a long haul.

Many friends have told me, "I don't know how you did it."

How did I endure months of chemotherapy and thirteen surgeries? You do what you have to do—especially when you are a mama bear who has to look out for her cubs. I never left porridge for Goldilocks. I ate it all, because I needed my strength. I guess that's what got me out of my size 2 jeans, come to think of it.

During one of my weekly meltdowns, I was sitting on the floor of my shower, crying and watching the last of my hair flow down the drain. I felt empty. I was now hairless all over, except my legs. GO FIGURE. I still couldn't escape shaving my legs! That felt like the universe giving me a red-nailed middle-finger. But then I picked myself up, got dressed, put my $300 squirrel on my head, and went to work.

Mental fortitude is a raw necessity when you are facing tough times, and strength comes from a deep place within.

You just have to keep going.

It turns out the saying "kids are resilient" is also true. Mine are young adults now, and if you ask them about this time in their life, they will most likely say they don't remember much except "Mom wearing a wig and being tired." Oh, and that we ate Stouffer's frozen macaroni and cheese for months. It was the only thing I liked to eat, and when Mom is happy, everyone is happy—and also eating mac and cheese.

My kids survived my illness. I think they are more compassionate people because of my struggles. They have learned to adapt to situations outside of their control. As a mom, I have learned that doing my best in the time of crisis was good enough.

Dating after cancer has proven to be an interesting endeavor.

We are all imperfect beings, cancer or not. As a middle-aged woman (GULP), it isn't easy to be "out there" in the dating world. The scars on my chest look like I had a boxing bout with Freddy Krueger; that did nothing to boost my self-confidence. But I decided to put my profile up on a dating site.

Still bald at that time, I donned my wig for my pictures. For months, that hair was my safety blanket. When you're bald, you always feel like you're standing naked in front of a crowd. Having super-short hair after cancer made me feel like I was standing in front of a group of cat-calling men wearing a thong. Me in the thong, not the men. Although that would be pretty funny.

After chatting with one man online, I uploaded a picture of myself with short hair. He asked me why I had cut it, and I reluctantly explained that I'd recently had cancer. I will never forget what he said next.

"The thought of dating someone who has had cancer is daunting to me. Good luck."

I wrote back, "Well, the thought of dating someone who could get hit by a bus is daunting to me. Make sure you look both ways before you cross the street. Oh, and good luck!"

First of all—what a dick! But second—and more important to share—is that this exchange shut me down for months. MONTHS! I felt completely alone and just plain horrible about myself. I decided never to allow this to happen to me again.

I have since realized that I can only control my own behavior. If some jackass feels the need to make a stupid comment, that's his problem. "Not my circus, not my monkey."

Now my story is out. I wrote a book about my journey and then started a non-profit organization to help cancer patients. If a prospective date Googles me, the unvarnished truth is there for him to see. I let it all hang out. Why not? I'm not ashamed of being a cancer survivor.

Cancer isn't the scarlet letter C. To me, it is a badge of honor.

I never went to war, but my body went to war with me—and I won. Although this cancer journey of mine was riddled with taxing times, I have grown from the experience. Change, no matter how uncomfortable it might feel in the beginning, can also be a good thing.

I know now that I am stronger than I ever imagined. Now I can look adversity right in the eye and tell it to "Back off!" We cannot let circumstances define us. Cancer was part of my life's journey, but it was never who I am. I'm a strong woman, a great mom, an entrepreneur, and many other things that define me as a person.

I am me—changed, but more powerful and improved. I have conquered many obstacles in my life. Cancer is just one of them.

I am grateful to have learned about living my life in the moment. That was the positive lesson of cancer.

As a planner, I know that you can't always plan your life. Some things are out of your control, and you just need to let them happen. But you can always learn a lesson.

When the time is right, my Prince Charming will appear, and we will trot off together into the sunset. Until then, I'm going to enjoy being right where I am.

Self-Healing, Wisdom, and the Infinite

by Tamee Knox

*With the desperate desire to thrive, eat, and regain physical strength,
I took an oath to focus on the deepest aspects of life.*

My body was in extreme pain. Severely exhausted and unable to eat, I'd lost enough weight to become gravely concerned. But then, the most incredible and miraculous thing happened. Now I am alive and well to tell you my story of change.

In my early forties, after some highly stressful life situations, many health and autoimmune issues struck me. I was weak from having eight miscarriages before finally giving birth to my second beautiful child. In addition to the emotional and physical distress, I had an extreme hormonal imbalance. My divorce, although I had initiated it, caused me great sadness, because I'd had so much hope in our lasting love. My body and soul were tired.

Over the next five years, my health changed rapidly for the worse. My body was deteriorating.

A multitude of unexplained symptoms and unresolved health issues kept me from enjoying the things I had once loved. Even simple activities became impossible. I felt sad and confused that I couldn't heal.

Because of food allergies and sensitivities, I was only able to consume between fifteen and twenty different foods. My diet consisted of egg yolks, a few types of beans, meat, bone and vegetable broths, apples, carrots, cashew butter, lettuce, onions, garlic, salt, and safflower oil. That's what I ate every day, for every meal. Cheating launched a cascade of reactions with dramatic consequences, from rashes and shortness of breath to exhaustion and migraines.

As life continued, so did my pain. I was weary of being ill and unable to resolve my many health issues. When conventional medical doctors examined me, they ordered the usual battery of tests, but they were unable to arrive at a diagnosis. Many doctors looked completely baffled.

The naturopathic doctors were stumped as well. Once a conventional female medical doctor listened to my woes and told me about spiritual healing. This surprised me, but it was little help at the time.

My desperate goals were to thrive, eat, and regain physical strength. Finally, too weak to shower, too exhausted to walk, and in too much pain to take a simple breath, I turned to the things I knew best: silence and meditation. This time, I didn't just need some quiet time to recover from an intense workout. This time I required a profound connection to my mind, body, and spirit—and to make a priority of recovering and getting my joy back.

The healing journey that changed my life started with trust and wisdom. I dove right into following divine intervention, trusting that the information coming through to me was love at its highest point—love both sacred and profound. Recognition, acceptance, and awareness of what is helped me initiate a communion with Spirit. I embarked on the path to infinite wisdom and radical acceptance and experienced transformation.

I vowed to focus on the deepest aspects of life through breath, sound, consciousness, vibration, nature, water, and prayer/inner wisdom. For energy and healing, I would have to learn how to appreciate these essential-but-immense energy systems, and to tap into each one's unique vibration.

I had to learn how to "live on the light," to get nourishment from sound (singing bowls /tuning forks), breath (practices to move, create, and store chi), nature (plants, insects, animals, minerals), sun (colors of light and their spectrums), water, mediations, prayer, and scalar energy-healing modalities.

These became daily practices, infusing me with familiar vibrations to be used on a whole new level. Because my one purpose was to get my life back, the daily practices became essential and sacred. I realized connecting with this energy was healing, if only for a moment.

Striking a sound bowl or humming a sound while lying down to embrace a relaxing breath, helped my body take on a form that bypassed the mind, with all its labels for feeling sick and its preoccupation with chronic illness. As my daily practice grew stronger, so did my desire to connect with other sacred energies. I read and researched endlessly on self-healing—everything from astrology and numerology to detox, NLP (Neuro-Linguistic Programming), mind science, bio geometry, bioenergetics, and more.

I kept practicing, investigating, and believing that one day, I would have strength again to walk and enjoy nature fully. I'd even be able to eat a variety of foods.

I didn't understand why I'd developed a sensitivity to so many foods. I still remembered the times when I could eat any food, in any amount, and it would not cause a negative reaction. I decided to concentrate on food in my meditations and other practices, especially my favorite foods: avocado, red pepper, and olive oil.

By becoming quiet and still, I could trust what my higher Self was leading me to do.

I would engage in Earth energies and play sound bowls with food and pictures of food by my side or in my lap. A specific food might accompany me into mediations, where I asked for guidance. I would carry a problematic food in my pocket, alongside gems and spiritual symbols labeled with prayers and words like "love," "forgive," "accept," and "I'm sorry." Every day, I did something to create a sacred union between myself, my cells, the spaces between my cells, and the food. My highest goal was to forge a sacred union with Divinity, a sacred trust and sacred wisdom.

One night, I was awakened by the voice of a familiar spirit: my twin flame's mother. In my twilight-sleep, she whispered the words, "Sally sighs, Sally, sighs." After recording her message in my journal, I went back to sleep. From that morning onward, whenever I awoke—and during the following eight months in meditation—I would ask, "Why is Sally sighing? Why is she sad?" The phrase drew me to look deeper into grief and fear, and to delve into past lives, multiple dimensions, unconditional love, and twin-flames—along with the energy practices I had been exploring.

The Kabbalah describes twin flames as "the other half of one's soul." They reunite to engage the spiritual awareness of their community of family, work, and friends.

I'd had visions of my twin flame for years, but we didn't meet in person until two months after his mother's death. Once we had met, his mom would come to me in meditations and dreams, to deliver messages for him concerning work, life, family, and unconditional love. Through this connection, the three of us became a "unit." We became a space for Divinity to stream through as dreams, visions, sacred messages, and infinite knowing.

Many months after my "Sally sighs" dream, I reached a turning point.

Truth, trust, acceptance, divine wisdom, and healing merged into one. Consciousness, oneness, and awareness … my opportunity was here. This was my chance to trust what was staring me deep in the eye. My opportunity to connect to the Divine was pulling me like never before.

I found myself gazing at a research paper on food allergy and salicylate sensitivity. The words of my twin flame's mother returned to me. She had whispered "Sally sighs." Was this a nudge from the other side? Did "SALY SIGH" LATE mean salicylate sensitivity?

Am I crazy? No way! But after reading many articles and books, I finally understood what had been contributing to so many of my health issues and symptoms: salicylates.

Many foods contain salicylates. Someone sensitive to them can have both physical and emotional reactions. Mine included sinus infection/pressure, gut issues, migraines, hot skin rash, shortness of breath, anxiety, exhaustion, muscle weakness, sensitive bladder, joint pain, loss of memory, confusion, lack of concentration, and more. Sometimes, these symptoms happened all at once.

As I began to process and accept this information, I tapped into infinite wisdom to make the necessary changes in my life. If this was a food sensitivity issue, it would be possible to heal and recover from the "dis-ease" by doing a detox and cleanses to improve my immune system and heal my gut. My changes even went as deep as removing the energetic imprints that the foods and symptoms had left. Over time, I slowly reintroduced the correct foods for my healing. It worked.

After my understanding of the "Sally sighs" dream, I returned to my doctor complaining of night sweats and a red, itchy rash all over my arms. "I think my salicylate sensitivity is related to my celiac disease," I said. She ordered a new set of blood tests. I then returned to my naturopathic doctor for alternative testing. A saliva test again confirmed celiac. Finally! The information from my dream had led to a true diagnosis. Celiac, IBS, and salicylates. When the body is stressed or celiac is active, salicylate sensitivity can increase.

Divine intervention is always at play.

Self-healing requires consciousness, awareness, trust, wisdom, practice, patience, balance, and determination. It's how you connect with the Divine that matters most. Sometimes, the most powerful intervention is accepting what is—even though it's not what you want or expected. Connecting with breath and sound can elevate you to the most profound treasures: healing and wisdom.

Today, I am thankful for my health. I can breathe without issues and move my body freely, as well as eat and enjoy the delicious foods that now help to keep me healthy.

There may be times in your life when the opportunity for change comes along, and you know you must take it. Somehow, some way, you trust yourself enough to dive right in and get immersed in it. This action is called wisdom, and for one to be wise, the trust and acceptance of *what IS* must grab you by the heart and lead you to unknown places. All of this is especially true for self-healing.

If you need to address a health issue, first focus on love and acceptance. Next, start diving in: diving into yourself through self-care and self-love and self-trust. Explore breath and sound on many levels. Continue to be wise and look to infinite wisdom, unconditional love, nature, water, sun, sacred geometry, inner silence, and rest.

I wish you many blessings on your journey to transformation, health, and healing.

How My Hope Was Born from Despair
by Maria Lehtman

Hope may be born from the most adverse circumstances. You can take away privacy and even dignity yet, hope lingers on.

A dark being stands silently next to me during my physiotherapy appointment. As a lucid dreamer, nothing seems strange to me and I wonder aloud, "What is Death doing here?"

My therapist, a compassionate soul who can pick up signals that some might call divine or paranormal, says, "Oh, I think he's just one of your teachers."

I address the being in my mind. "Is my number up?"

"No," he replies. "Your number is not up." The answer echoes in my thoughts.

"That's good," I say. "Thank you." Relieved, I dismiss Death from my mind.

Later, I will come to regret not sharing this dialogue with my husband. He is a grounded, no-nonsense man, but he trusts my intuition. If Death had said my number was not up, he felt I should have mentioned it.

A month later, things begin to change.

For two weeks, my husband has been suffering from a mild cold, and I finally catch it. My throat hurts and I'm feverish and completely drained of energy. The next day, I feel worse. I visit a doctor, who brushes me off without ordering any blood tests or writing a prescription. Off I go, carrying a three-day sick-leave note. With my problematic IBS (Irritable Bowel Syndrome), I know I'm likely to need much more time, but I feel too exhausted to argue.

Four days later, after coughing day and night, I cough up a bright red smear of blood. I call my husband at work and ask him to take me back to the doctor. He asks if I can hold on for two more hours—but then, after hearing something raspy in my voice, he changes his mind. He summons an ambulance and phones a family member to ride with me to the hospital.

I am certain his decision saved my life.

When my husband gets to the hospital, he finds me in intensive care—in a medically induced coma. My CRP (C-reactive protein) levels, which should be below three milligrams per liter, are over 600. That means my immune system is failing to fight off the invading bacteria.

I have severe blood poisoning and pneumonia.

The doctors won't give my husband much comfort. They can only say that the next days will show if my IV antibiotics will help. They won't guarantee that my internal organs will survive blood poisoning.

I am already frail, weighing 101.2 pounds (46 kilograms). Being 20 percent below a normal body weight, it's is a miracle that I was able to walk to the ambulance. My oxygen intake is 30 percent, and I am covered in masks and tubes. I had been suffocating from the phlegm in my lungs without even realizing it.

For three nights and days, my husband is uncertain if he'll ever see me awake again. He blames himself for not taking me to the hospital sooner. Finally, a nurse informs him that it looks like I will pull through, but I'll have to stay in the coma until the worst is over.

I am fully immersed in a near-death experience (NDE).

While my body lies motionless in the hospital bed, my soul is journeying in full battle mode through the despair of the shadow world. I traverse lucid stages of consciousness, from one war zone to another. Sometimes, I am sentenced to death—but then I'm commanded to fight another mission.

I experience missions throughout history, from 1600 BC to 2300 AD, where I'm tortured and held hostage. I bargain for freedom, escape, and infiltrate enemy lines. Then I'm captured again, only to appear magically on another timeline, fighting another mission. My goal is to protect my family, release as little information as possible, and return to my husband in the current timeline.

There is one defining moment, my ultimate NDE test.

It is 2317 AD in Antarctica, and I'm with a small search party that includes my husband. We're hiking to the North Pole, an area some people call the New Zion. Since I'm exhausted beyond measure, my husband eventually has to pull me in a sled. It is snowing, and the freezing wind is whipping my body.

When we finally arrive, we're suddenly ambushed by the same enemy group I have escaped from multiple times. They raid our campsite and capture everyone. Food is scarce, and their only aim is to quell their agonizing hunger. I hear the screams of people being roasted alive as I grow weaker. The raiders recognize me. They give me enough attention to keep me alive.

I want to die. I am exhausted in every way a human being can be. My husband, always the optimist, leans toward me from time to time to ask if I need anything. I only need to escape. He'll be at risk if they find out how much I know about them, but he loves me too much to let me go. My life begins to trickle away from me. I can feel the sensation of death in every part of my body.

But then: A miracle! An intervention. Another group invades the camp. In the commotion, I push myself upward and find myself in a high-altitude, low-pressure atmosphere. Kicking my legs to go higher into space, I ascend toward a sky that's deep black and clear, filled with brilliant stars. I am so cold. I call ahead to my Heavenly Father and say, "I am coming back."

After the Gates of Heaven refuse to take me in, I return home.

Cold and hot waves shiver through my body as I find myself on my elevated hospital bed. A doctor asks, "Do you know where you are?"

Duh, that's fairly obvious, I want to say. I calmly answer, "In the hospital."

"Which hospital, and how long do you think you've been here?"

Oh, a tougher question. I can recall hallucinations or dreams of being transferred to two hospitals, so I venture a guess—but it's wrong. I don't know where I am. Strike one for Team Patient.

"One or two days, perhaps …" I answer. Strike two.

"You have been here for one and a half weeks. Some of that time, you were in a coma. Your blood levels look better now, but we're going to keep you here until you're stronger."

My agitated mind is reeling with disbelief! Later, when speaking with my husband, I realize I have no recollection of the past two weeks. I can't recall standing outside in the cold with my hospital bag, waiting for the ambulance, or how the paramedics tried to make me breathe into a mask while driving me to the emergency room. I have no idea that they slashed my sweater open to get me ready for the orchestration of tubes.

My pain is finally down to a bearable level. And I'm home.

I have been regaining muscle strength, one painful day after another, and a little weight: up to only 97 pounds (44 kilograms), but that's more than when I was discharged from the hospital. I can finally drive a car once a week for small errands. Returning to work keeps my mind from thinking about my four-month recovery period.

It has been a year now, and I have gained 22 pounds (10 kilograms). I work full-time from home. I love my writing and photography. My family and my work community keep me going. I've returned to singing in a choir, the only live community in which I have the energy to participate.

My search continues for communities who understand what a complete self-transformation means. I read about other people who have experienced NDE, and realize we have one thing in common: No one comes back from a near-death experience unchanged.

A person with my name went into a coma, but another person emerged after a fundamental transformation. Western healthcare calls these transcendental and even religious experiences "dreams or hallucinations." I've never felt I needed therapy to cope with what happened to me, but I do think there should be a peer group to help family members accept a patient transformed by NDE.

I have met a few other people who have experienced NDE. Like me, they are convinced they crossed to the life hereafter and explored a dimension between life and death. Almost dying was the ultimate test of my hope.

This new hope and reality are going strong.

Now my dreams are in 4-D, accompanied by all the sensations a body can feel. The pain brought me a gift. I know that to learn the full spectrum of hope, one has to endure utter despair. I no longer fear death. Life is a journey. Most of all, my life is an opportunity to learn to love and spread hope.

I am so thankful for my loving husband, my best friend, who has become my biggest fan and ally. He has been there to support me and my dreams. I know that the universe and my husband patiently guided me back to life. He sat beside my hospital bed every single night and spoke to my higher Self: "If you exist, you'd better stop your universal explorations and park your bod in this chair until my wife is back!"

I suppose she believed him.

Never stop giving people hope when they need it most—even if they don't know it.

Never let go of life.

Shift Your Focus for Change
By Eileen Bild

*Sometimes our mind overrides our inner compass
and we fail to see what is right there.*

I suffer from a debilitating condition known as fibromyalgia. The chronic symptoms eventually forced me to rock bottom, robbing me of my energy and zest for life.

Being close to the ocean has always been cathartic for me, and this time, I was there for contemplation and comfort. The salt air surrounding my body was healing my tears as I strolled through the neighborhood, feeling a deep desire for change and a need to rehabilitate my mind, body, and spirit.

My sister walked beside me. She was a source of warmth as she tried to console my anguish. But I was overwhelmed with tears—frustrated, angry, and exasperated. But even as my hopelessness seemed unbearable, it was engaging my will to find a solution.

Each morning, I found ways to drag myself out of bed, function throughout my day, and then do it all again. For more than seven years, I had forced myself to be there for my family as best I could.

I might have looked normal from the outside, but inside, I felt like a train wreck that would be impossible to repair.

On my last night at the beach, I was worn out, emotionally and physically. With barely enough energy to take a bite of food—in excruciating pain, and with my brain fog at its peak—I surrendered. I had worked so hard to get answers from doctors and treatment for the symptoms. But my search for healing had been fruitless. The fight was over now. I felt I had only one option: to stop trying to make it stop.

Then, from deep within, a powerful force beyond my control came spiraling up. My fists pumped toward the sky as I shouted, *"Take me or heal me! I am not doing this anymore!"*

A significant shift rocked my world.

That declaration marked the start of my road to recovery. After returning home, magic started happening. It seemed that people and serendipitous experiences were mysteriously shifting into place.

The synchronicities were mind-boggling. I began to reunite with old friends who became instrumental in my healing. An introduction to new ways of thinking and *being* suddenly emerged in my life, seemingly out of nowhere. Both my sense of who I was, and my life purpose came into focus. Now I could see where I had been weak and naïve. My head was reeling with all the information coming at me faster than I could absorb it.

What was going on?

Since my childhood, people have opened up to me about their lives, without my invitation. They will tell me, "I have never said this to anyone, but…." and continue to purge whatever was on their mind.

When my healing began to make a difference in how I was feeling, and my ability to lead a more normal life started to take shape, I felt a pull to do something of importance; something that would have a positive impact on others. Not knowing what this could be, following life nudges and golden nuggets became a part of my new direction.

During a life coaching session, the "Aha!" moment occurred.

Have you ever noticed that sometimes our mind overrides our inner compass and we fail to see what is right there? Well, one day while I was creating a life-purpose statement with my coach, my inner compass had something to say. Words that were foreign to my consciousness came through me, presenting me in a way I'd never considered. It was surreal.

The no-brainer answer I was casually writing suddenly was translated into a totally different language. It felt as if, although I was composing a statement with my mind, my soul wanted to tell a different story. When I put the pen down and read what I'd written, a moment of pure stillness and silence enveloped me. I had to read it over and over to fully grasp what had just happened.

The words said, *"I am a guiding light to show people the way."*

I saw a vivid image of a lighthouse whose radiance guides the ships at night, to keep them from crashing against the rocky shore. The change from sickness to health had been the turning point. Now I understood I was meant to follow my own path in developing ways to be of service to others. My first business, Serenity Expressions, was born.

Over the years, I've learned many lessons and developed a greater understanding of why things happen. Although I would have preferred never having to go through the trauma of fibromyalgia, I now see that illness was a necessary piece of the puzzle. This realization has given me the drive and the tools to be who I am today.

In hindsight, the threads of what I am seeking—and what is seeking me—have ever-so-slowly become interwoven. Life is the master teacher. Each experience has given me more courage to face myself in times of struggle and to determine what needs to be done differently.

To be in the world, but not of it, is the challenge.

When I focus on my eyes in the mirror, what do I see? The image staring back at me is complex and deep. There is a sense of triumph, but also a winding road to travel. There is recognition of a greatness that encompasses all that I am, and yet also an awareness that I am an individual part of this whole.

I have evolved by assisting others to reach their highest potential. I teach people things I learned through my suffering and healing. When life tests my truth and makes me question what I think I know, a part of me remembers my declaration and subsequent life-purpose statement.

No matter what my thoughts, actions, or responses may be, and no matter what comes into my experience, I strongly believe that tomorrow is another day and another opportunity. This thought gives me inner peace and serenity. I also learn a great deal from my clients, as they are a reflection of me.

Today, I have what I call "hiccups" rather than hard punches.

The present is not the defining moment or the final accomplishment. Instead, I view the present moment as a continuous enhancement of what has risen. Each moment is like a glorious phoenix rising out of the ashes from full-blown destruction, which implodes and then explodes into something extraordinary.

Additional changes and shifts have manifested in ways I could never have imagined. I am now inspired to write morning musings that seem to have a positive impact, sometimes even saving lives. When someone tells me that my writing has had a powerful impact, I smile, knowing I am making a difference—even if it is just for one person at a time.

I feel grateful and fulfilled now with a discernment of what makes life worth living. Whatever happens is between me and the Greater Source beyond my vision, which is holding my hand as I sojourn across the threshold from one day to the next, guiding me to be the best I can be.

Two Words
by Mel Greenberg

Surviving my worst nightmare liberated me.

It was a hot day in July. It was much like any other summer day in Tucson—until it wasn't.

"*Spiculated margins,*" my doctor said, and those two little words forever made this day different from every other. These were words I hadn't heard before, but they would soon become as much a part of my vocabulary as hello and goodbye.

On this hot summer day, I had a routine mammogram—something I'd done religiously since my late twenties. The film revealed a tiny mass. I looked down at the screen, staring till I lost focus, and then glanced up at my doctor's face. Her concern, and the empathy in her expression, revealed a truth her words did not. Those *spiculated margins* were a potential problem we'd have to investigate further.

A biopsy would determine what, if any, action was needed.

My doctor looked worried, even though she didn't say, she couldn't say.

She knew …

I knew …

She said I should try not to worry. But I did worry! I had worried for as long as I could remember, since long before those two little words took on a life of their own. Before the biopsy, the diagnosis, the medical team, the plan, and the treatment, there had been a seventeen-year-old girl.

I had been that girl, filled with fear, a broken heart, and so many memories. I'd been not quite an adult, not quite ready to be tossed out into the world alone.

But that's precisely what happened. Life happened. And with a few words—softly spoken in a sterile office on a hot summer day, thirty-two years later—I was there again. My thoughts wandered off as I mulled over what my future might look like—and remembered my past.

Mom's story ended on July 14, 1977, after a brief, hard-fought battle with the formidable opponent.

She'd kept most of the details from me: the diagnosis, the extent of the disease living within her, and the dire prognosis. She would be fine, she'd say. She would beat it. Don't worry. I didn't, or at least, not overtly—though I was aware that things were not as they used to be. But they were our days, and Mom was there as much as she could be.

She was there with love, supporting me, watching over me, being a mom. I'd been unaware of just how much life knowledge and strength she tried to infuse into our daily lives, preparing me to carry on without her. I didn't know just how soon that day would arrive.

I can only speculate about what she endured and why she made the decisions she did. It took becoming a mother myself to understand her motivation to suffer alone, to keep me out of her day-to-day, physical and emotional struggles. It was less about bravery, I think, than about protecting a child from life's unexpected hardships. As a single mother, she did her level best to ensure that my teenage years would be complete with all the milestones and exciting times that define a young girl's passage into adulthood.

They were …

They are …

Somewhere between Mom saying, "Honey, I have breast cancer," and my doctor saying, "Try not to worry," I grew up.

I went to college, got a job and a husband, and became a mom. Life sometimes had its way with me, but I survived. I navigated through each stage of my adult life without her. To be honest, I felt a bit of resentment along the way. I was never one to spend a lot of time at the pity party, except when those milestones she had coveted popped up: graduation, marriage, and the births of my two sons. In the happy times, the memory-making times, I missed her.

I questioned it all, and somewhere along the way, my questions turned into fear—fear that my story would end as hers had, that cancer would find its way to me, and that I would die, just as she had. I convinced myself her sad journey might also be my destiny.

Early in my twenties, anxiety began to replace my ache for her loss. I found a sad sort of comfort in imagining that anytime I got sick, found a mole, or had a cough or a headache, the diagnosis would come. Then I could just accept my fate and get on with it.

What "it" was in those early days, I have no idea! Was it life or death I feared more? Likely a bit of both. I just wanted the worrying to stop.

It didn't …

And then it did …

I was only slightly younger than my mom had been when she'd lost her battle. Now I stood, pondering my future.

But then, something remarkable happened. Suddenly, the torment, panic, and angst were gone. I felt curiously empowered. A new source of strength saturated me. Positive, active energy surged through my body and spirit.

During the days that followed—as I told my family the news and put together my medical team—I remember experiencing a complete release. What I'd dreaded for so long—the single worst thing I could imagine that might happen to me—*did* happen. And I was OKAY. I would be OKAY!

The diagnosis, and my choices about how to process it and proceed with it all, were a blessing.

I gained a perspective that might never have been possible otherwise. The life I'd been given, the family I'd created, and the things I'd accomplished appeared in a new light.

Before I got cancer, I spent my days fretting the *what-ifs*.

After I got cancer, my thoughts shifted to the *what-nows*.

I'd spent so much of my life just getting through—overcoming tremendous challenges, experiencing successes, and carrying on the best I could. Through it all, I kept my anxious, obsessive inner dialogues private. On the surface, it looked like I'd been raising my family and engaging my life. But just beneath mumbled the incessant, nervous ramblings of my inner voice, the night sweats, and the absurd notion that I could somehow control whatever my destiny was to be.

My diagnosis taught me that the only thing I could control was my response.

That was perhaps my most significant takeaway. It's a perception for which I am eternally grateful.

I was blessed …

I am blessed …

In just a few weeks, I'll celebrate my *tenth* birthday. It's been three thousand, six hundred fifty days since those two little words—*spiculated margins*—entered my life and changed it forever.

"My life!" Those two big *new* words have become my mantra.

Saying them reaffirms my faith in the journey.

My life is now defined by two other big words: *before* and *after*.

Before the diagnosis, I had a good life, a well-intentioned and meaningful life. But its course was off. My energy was misspent. Hope was conditional. I knew life could be better, but not how to get there.

Before …

After …

Now I know. I am grateful for the years spent agonizing, in terror that cancer would take my life. In fact, it gave my life back to me, and I embraced this new life with open arms. I always have choices in how to live each day, regardless of what comes at me.

My direction has changed considerably over this past decade. I've become an empty nester. I found a new career by returning to an old passion, and I rediscovered my voice along the way. And I am now, and will forever be, a cancer *"survivor."* I like that.

Surviving my worst nightmare liberated me.

This was my sign. I was done being afraid, done with spending my time fretting about the unknown. It's *all* unknown, after all.

And I really like the new me! I'm not afraid of anything now: not new directions, opportunities, or challenges. My satisfaction and joy come from seeing just how seamlessly I can navigate life's inevitable, changing tide. Now I'm grateful to be able to welcome back, with open arms, the frightened young girl who had disappeared in her teens. She hadn't been ready for the tumultuous road ahead.

But me? I am ready. Ready to live.

To be free …

I am free …

Men Have Breasts, Too
by Peggy Miller

No man will ever feel alone when hearing the words,
"You have breast cancer."

The end of April 2003 was the beginning of a scary chapter in our lives.

Our second son, Bret, was finishing his junior year in high school when he came upstairs and said, "Hey, Mom and Dad, what do you think this is?"

As he showed us a lump under his right nipple, in the back of my mind, I immediately thought, "Oh, my God! Could this be the type of lump they preach to us women to check for in our breasts?"

His dad replied, "It's nothing. I get them all the time."

We were self-employed and could not afford health insurance, but I knew Physical Night was coming up the first week of May. The parents at the high school who were doctors donated their time to do physical exams for just twenty-five dollars per student athlete. Bret was a football player and a wrestler, so he was eligible. I wanted him to have the lump checked.

Of course, Bret said, "Mom, it will be embarrassing if I ask them to check my nipple at school!"

I assured him that he would be in a private examination room. He agreed to the school check-up *if* the lump was still there. It was, and on Physical Night, Bret showed it to the doctor.

"Wait here," the doctor said. He returned with five other physicians to inspect Bret's nipple.

Their conclusion? The breast lump was caused by puberty. He was becoming a man!

Fast-forward to Bret's college physical exam, one year later. The examining doctor had the same opinion about the lump: Bret was healthy. We believed what the doctors told us.

When Bret graduated from college four years later, everything was excellent. He had a fantastic job managing the swimming and ice hockey teams at the private country club where he'd worked since he was fourteen. As a full-time employee, he finally had health insurance. He also still had the lump.

"It would be smart to have another doctor check that out," I said.

He got an appointment with a doctor whose practice specialized in men. As Bret was running out the door to the doctor's office, I yelled at him, "Make sure you ask the doctor about that lump, or I will send your ass right back to him!"

Bret had developed a new symptom. He'd told his dad about it but had failed to mention it to me. For more than a year and a half, he'd been noticing a yellow-orange discharge coming out of his right nipple. His dad had told him to "shake it off."

If Bret had given that information to a woman in his life, we would have gotten him immediate medical attention!

Bret got a thorough physical, and the doctor said everything looked great. As he was walking out the door of the examining room, he remembered my words. He showed the doctor his breast lump.

The doctor said, "I don't think it is anything, but I'll send you for a sonogram."

Two days later, at the sonogram, the technician summoned several doctors into the room. They immediately sent him for a mammogram. Bret told the mammogram technician, "I didn't know you could do *that* on MEN!"

When he returned home, he told me, "I have a whole new respect for women now. How can you stand those mammograms?"

The mammography results showed Bret needed an immediate biopsy. Although Bret was now a twenty-four old man, no longer a high school boy, he was still *our* boy, so we accompanied him to the procedure.

The day of the biopsy, I told my husband, "I do not like that doctor!" It turns out the doctor had been told to "never touch another breast patient." Yet, somehow, we still got him.

We knew the biopsy results would be available when Bret was busy at work, so he signed HIPAA papers allowing the doctor to call us with the results first. Then we would let Bret know them. Well, that didn't happen.

Bret was driving from the country club to his bartending job downtown when the doctor called. He didn't even ask Bret if he was in a safe place to talk.

"Hey, Bret, I wanted to let you know you have breast cancer," the doctor said. "You will need to have a mastectomy."

Bret called his dad and said, "Please don't tell Mom yet, but the doctor called. I have breast cancer."

My husband Bob hung up the phone and said nothing, but he was red in the face. He didn't need to tell me.

I said, "That was Bret, and he has breast cancer."

Bob said, "Yes, but he is on the way to work. We'll talk tonight when he gets home."

When Bret walked in the door at four a.m., I asked him, "In a man's physical exam, don't they check your breasts?"

"They check our butts and our nuts, but not our chest," he said. "That would be weird!"

That was my Oprah "Aha!" moment. We need to change the way the medical profession handles this.

One month later, Bret was scheduled for his mastectomy. The news stations here in Kansas City picked up the story. The morning of the surgery, I prayed with Bret so hard. We asked God and St. Jude to please help him get well. I promised to build awareness of male breast cancer for the rest of my life.

Right after Bret's diagnosis, he had said, "Mom, I want to set up a foundation, because it took so long for me to get diagnosed. I don't want any other man to go through what I had to." He also promised his surgeon, "No man will ever feel alone when hearing the words, 'You have breast cancer.'"

That day, I went online and started the Bret Miller 1T Foundation— and the rest is history. We chose the name for the foundation because Bret has one T in his name, and one tit and one nipple now.

God answered our prayers and continues to answer them. I am forever grateful.

Bret has been working at the country club now for nineteen years. He got married in 2018. The doctors had told him he might never be able to father children because he'd had extensive chemotherapy, but my first grandbaby—Ms. Riley Sue—was born July 13, 2019.

We are a blessed family. Bret is now a nine-year male breast cancer survivor. He's happily married, and now he's a miracle-father.

Final Thoughts

Illness can be an incredible teacher who illuminates our strengths, weaknesses, limitations, and self-reliance. Its chaos can slow us down and give us the time needed to mend, emotionally and physically, by forcing us to reevaluate our priorities—because life does not always proceed as expected.

A thread of wisdom woven through the stories in this section is that, no matter how much the body is abused or attacked, it can restore balance and find its way back to health and wellness—and even thrive. Inner guidance can be our best friend, standing by us through the worst of the storm, walking with us toward the light of clarity.

More than 2,000 years ago, the ancient Greek philosopher Aristotle said, "Happiness is a broad term that describes the experience of positive emotions, such as joy, contentment, and satisfaction." Emerging research[1] shows that, not only does happiness feel good, but it also brings with it a host of potential health and wellness benefits. Happier is healthier.

Healthy relationships also can help us during times of great sadness, as seen in the next section of true stories, *Grief and Loss: Let the Circle Be Unbroken.*

PART 3

GRIEF AND LOSS
Let the Circle Be Unbroken

What if we choose to
Be the Light
In another's darkness?
Hold space
For another's pain?
Be a balm
On another's wound?
Be comfortable
In our uncomfortableness
For another?

Love Never Dies
by Kathleen O'Keefe-Kanavos

Death is the Great Changer. After Death, nothing is the same except Love, because Love never dies.

The moon was full the night my mother died. The colon cancer won as she silently surrendered her battered body during that special time between two and four a.m. known as the Hour of Souls; different from the Witching Hour of midnight.

Mom often described The Hour of Souls as the time souls chose to free themselves of their worldly bodies. As a nurse, Mom had seen it happen. The Hour of Souls was indeed a special time for death.

After the dreadful 3:30 a.m. phone call from the hospital, I sit outside on my deck chair in the dark, numb with grief. I hug my knees to my chest and rock for comfort until my nagging questions transform into a solid knot in the pit of my stomach.

Had Mom chosen to die during this hour, or did it just happen? Do we have control over our time of death, or do we suddenly find ourselves in a dream from which we cannot awaken, unaware that we've died? Most important—are we alone, confused, and frightened as we leave our bodies behind?

Hearing no answers, I turn those thoughts inward to my weeklong emotional blindness. All the signs of impending death had stared me in the face, but I had missed them. I had ignored Death waving to me from the distance. Would I have done things differently tonight if I had paid attention to or understood those unearthly signals as messages from the other side? Mom had seen those signs, as had her nurse. Only I had been blind to Death.

Where are you, Mom, really? Where are you right now? The words scream in my mind as much to myself as to her. I didn't want to think, *She's in a better place in heaven, with God and Jesus, blah, blah, and blah …*

My emotions had reached a crescendo of confusion compounded by grief and immense guilt because of those questions asked in the dark. *What kind of daughter would pray for her mother's death? Did I do this to Mom with my nightly prayers begging God to either heal her or take her? Was Mom's death the power of prayer, the circle of life, or both?*

Would a Higher Power actually listen to someone as insignificant as me? *You are using this "God thought" to distract yourself from the true question at hand and let yourself off the hook,* I mentally berate myself. *Stay focused! Answer the question! What kind of daughter would pray for her mother's death as soon as possible, now, tonight, or even yesterday?*

Hugging my legs even tighter while crying into my knees, I almost miss the voice that whispers the answer: "*A daughter whose love has no limits.*"

The words leave me motionless. Listening, I rotate in my chair and strain my eyes and ears to locate the elusive voice. Had I imagined it, or was someone else here? I need to speak to that voice because, right now, the "afterlife" seems like some pathetic fairytale.

Something critical was at stake: Mom's soul. "Mom! Where are you?" I whisper, eagerly listening for the voice in the breeze to speak again.

Silence.

"How could you leave me?" I ask.

We had spent so much time together while my military father traveled to countries and places too far or too dangerous for us to go. When we did follow, we were often the only source of comfort for each other. We both knew the feeling of being strangers in strange lands.

This was the life of a rootless Army brat. At least Mom and I had always had each other as friends. Surely Mom would answer me now, if she could. Was she now a stranger in a strange land—alone, confused, and looking for me as I called out to her?

Did Mom know she was dead?

How far away could she possibly be, with only an hour separating her from life? Then another question on life and death pushes its ugly head to the surface of my mind from the deepest, darkest depths of my grief. *If I died right now, could I catch up to her? Could I find Mom? Could we offer each other comfort?*

Stop that thought right now! I scold myself. *What are you thinking? Get a grip!*

I taught psychology at the University of South Florida, and know that particular question was dangerous, especially for someone consumed by grief.

My thoughts could get me locked away on suicide watch!

But I wasn't being suicidal—just painfully honest in my curiosity about this afterlife concept—right? I listen again for the elusive "voice" and wonder if it would also chide me for my dangerous curiosity, or if it might agree with me. But all I heard were crisp palm fronds rustling in the tropical breezes.

Maybe the answer to that self-destructive question was too dangerous for a mere mortal to hear. After all, it really was a lovely night to die.

As I blot the stream of tears from my face with the sleeve of my silk nightshirt, I notice the reflection of the luminous full moon shimmering in our swimming pool—so close and yet, like Mom, so far away. Could this moon connect Mom to me now?

In despair, I wonder if anything could ever connect us again, or if that part of our life was over forever. Would I really never again pick up a telephone and say, "Hey Mom, wanna get some lunch and chat?" The reality of this past-life in my present state makes me sick to my stomach. I sit perfectly still and will the waves of nausea to pass, afraid to even shift my eyes from the glow of the silvery moon. Regret enters the moment.

I should have been there to hold her hand when she died. The thought of her dying alone was more unbearable than the thought of her dying at all. She would never have let me die alone. The signs had all been there earlier in the evening, but I had chosen not to see them.

Was my absence fueled by my fear of death, or was it an unspoken agreement between us? Had it been, perhaps, a decision made before our births and only now remembered and played out so she could leave the Earth and I could let her go? Had the thought of losing my mother, a person I had adored all my life, been too terrifying for me to handle? Would watching her die before my eyes have destroyed me emotionally for life, or would the profound grief visible on my face the moment before her death have held her here on Earth past her time to go, prolonging her suffering?

The first sign that all was not well tonight was when Mom had told me there was a man in the hospital room watching her, a man no one else could see. She had refused to let the nurses undress her in front of him, clutching the sheets tightly around her frail body as she stared at an empty corner near the window at the foot of her bed. "It's a drug-induced hallucination," the nurses had whispered—a reaction to the pain medications in her IV drip. "We see it all the time."

"Mom, do you *know* the man at the foot of your bed?" I had asked her when we were alone. "Have you seen him before today? Does he talk to you?"

"No," She had answered clear as a bell to all three questions. "He just stands there and watches me. Look, he's there right now." She pointed with her nose, because both of her fragile, bruised arms were taped with multiple IVs—her lifelines to a dying cause.

I had been startled by an unrecognizable reflection in the dark window. It was mine. Dark circles were etched beneath my weary eyes. My ever-present dark sunglasses—an interchangeable headband and mask—perched atop my head. I never knew when I might need to flip them down to hide my tears, but that usually happened during a doctor's visit.

Whenever the doctor came into Mom's room and announced with a smile, "We'll clear up Mom's pneumonia and she'll be back home to resume chemotherapy in a week," I would flip down my dark sunglasses, slink off to the nearest bathroom, sit on a toilet seat while I wept as silently as possible.

Although I had searched for the Mom's mysterious man, no one stood at the foot of her bed.

Maybe I couldn't feel this mysterious visitor, despite my intuitive gifts, because all my emotional and psychic buttons had been dialed down low, so I could deal rationally with the present. However, the notion of this unseen man had conjured up new questions. *Is Mr. Invisible here to protect Mom, to take her from me, or to catch a ride with her if she goes to the "other side"?* Questions I instantly dismissed as too profound for my numbed mind to ponder.

I'll save those questions for another time when I can handle the answers.

I had suspected when I checked Mom into the hospital five days earlier that she would not check out in the conventional way. No loving family members would wheel her out to a car and finally to a comfy bed at home. I hadn't wanted to think about how and where she would finally be wheeled by strangers just doing their job. It wouldn't be warm and comfy.

Deep down, I had always suspected the doctor's predicted happy ending was not to be our reality. The invisible man in Mom's room had seemed to confirm this—but I had not been reading the signs. I had been in blind denial, unable to listen when Mom tried to tell me that her colon cancer was the only cancer that had ever been in our family. That conversation had taken place the day before.

"I don't know how much more time I have," she had murmured as she gently clasped my hand. She was lying on a cold gurney tucked against the hospital's corridor wall as she waited for an ultrasound to confirm what she already knew, but I had refused to accept: the degree to which her cancer had metastasized.

During her procedure, Mom had intently watched for my reaction. I had flipped down my sunglasses. I didn't want her to feel more pain by watching me suffer through her ultrasound. The test had confirmed that her sands of time were down to a few stubborn grains that clung to the side of the hourglass.

Back in her room, as I helped the nurse change Mom's soiled gown and bed sheets for the fifth time that evening, the nurse had asked me if I planned to stay the night.

"Stay the night?" I repeated. She knew my house was just five minutes away. But she had smiled a smile that comes from years of experience with death before continuing her rounds, which left me to ponder her question. I had wanted to believe I would see Mom again the next morning, to brush her hair and tuck a pillow behind her sore back, the same routine we had followed for the past five days.

So, as I applied a damp cloth to her closed eyes to reduce the glare from the fluorescent overhead lights, I had leaned over and kissed Mom goodnight, not believing it was goodbye. Despite the oxygen tube, her breathing was labored, so she slept in an upright, Buddha-like position and appeared to be in deep meditation. Looking back, it might have been deeper than meditation. Perhaps that was another sign I had missed. Now, in the glow of the full moon, I realize the nurse's question was sign number two.

The nurse and Mom had known what I refused to see. Death was riding closer.

After kissing Mom goodbye, I had returned home around eleven p.m., emotionally and physically exhausted. My husband was still in Tampa, working on an important business deal. Baby Cakes, our cat, had cuddled peacefully against me in bed, comforting me with his low purr while we watched Arnold Schwarzenegger in the movie *Predator* blast jungle trees to pieces with a portable Gatling gun.

Suddenly, three huge, dark shadows had slipped into my bedroom through the pool area's locked, sliding-glass door. They slid across the ceiling and flew down the hallway toward the room my mother had occupied for the past six weeks. The towering shadows had appeared to be on a mission, hunting for something or someone.

"What the hell was that?" I yelled, ducking beneath the covers.

Baby Cakes had jumped off the bed and slid across the marble floor, racing for my closet. *Nothing just flew around the room. There were no shadows on my ceiling*, I had told myself as I peered from the safety of my sheets. I know now that I should have leapt out of bed and raced back to the hospital. But I had still been immersed in denial, refusing to read the signs.

Peter had arrived home after midnight. "You saw what? Where? You're overtired, Bunny," he had said, calling me by my pet name. "Let me hold you until you fall asleep." He'd scoffed at my story of flying blobs. But when he thought I wasn't looking; he had peered down the hallway.

The shrill telephone had awakened us at 3:30 a.m. A female voice gently announced that my mother had lost her fight. Now, all the signs fit together like giant pieces of a Kindergarten jigsaw puzzle. They all made perfect sense: Mom's invisible visitor, the nurse asking me if I planned to stay the night, the Buddha pose, and the shadows on the ceiling. The signs had been there, but I hadn't been prepared to look Death in the face—even when Death tried to make eye contact.

However, it's impossible to ignore Death when it slaps you in the face.

Now, drunk with grief and fatigued from my endless mind-babble, I stagger back into bed from our pool and the light of the silvery moon. Again, I pull the covers protectively around me and return to my fetal position. Once settled into bed, I'm stunned, not by a voice this time, but by what feels like invisible arms reaching around me. Someone was snuggled against my back, "spooning" me. It was just the way I used to spoon against Mom as a frightened child in Berlin, Germany, seeking nightly protection from the sound of marching ghost-soldiers in our hallway. Their cigarette smoke and laughter had filled the corridor from the midnight Witching Hour to the Hour of Souls.

But tonight, in Florida, the smell of Mom's perfume as she presses against me gives me comfort. She is still in my life, but on that other plane— the world I had known during my childhood terrors and now often visited in my dreams. I encircle my own body with my arms, hoping Mom feels me hug her while she hugs me.

She has just answered all my tortured questions with one simple act of love from the "other side." Our souls will link us forever across time, space, and realms. I don't need the phone or the moon to connect us. If I listen, I will hear her.

If there are some things we can take with us, love must be one of them.

It's natural for parents to die before children. My mind, but not my heart, grasps the concept that parents die so their children can become fully independent and truly come into their own. Sixteen months after watching Mom die of colon cancer, I came into my own when I was diagnosed with breast cancer "that does not run in our family."

Would death now be my fate? Should I watch for the same signs I had so carefully ignored during Mom's last days? Would my questions about the shadows on my bedroom ceiling be answered when they came to search for me?

Will the moon be full the night I die?

The full moon became many things to me during my cancer treatment: my shield against uncertainty and a personal symbol for survival, but especially, a sign of my Mom's love. Any time I gazed at that glowing orb in the darkness of night or life, I would say under my breath, "Look, Mom, there's our moon." I know in my heart that she heard me and smiled as she watched me survive cancer three times.

The moon was so full the night my mother died, and her love lived on.

Horse Whisperer: Listen to Your Heart
by Helen Brennand

Everything we search for is hidden right here in existence.

December 21, 2012 was the memorable day our beautiful son Samson was delivered into the world. His motionless body was adorned with thick black hair, perfect features, and a tiny but powerful frame. The sheer strength that emanated from this small form held my gaze. His lifeless body did not represent sadness. It displayed the dignity and honor of the spirit that had once resided within it.

His right hand was placed upon his heart as the index finger of his left hand pointed to and touched his left ear. What a profound picture he showed me: a gift forever imprinted on my mind.

I knew my lifeless little boy was telling me to listen to my heart.

If I followed his subtle guidance, somehow, he would connect with me. He left me with the sense that we would never be parted. His message brought me great comfort and allowed me the space and strength to honor him.

We gently dressed Samson and laid his body in the special white box the midwife had brought, as I couldn't bear to leave him behind in the hospital's clinical environment. We wanted to show him how loved he was and share with him what would have been his home. I longed to tell him of all our hopes and aspirations, the things we had planned for his budding life.

My first port of call had to be the horses that bring us such joy.

We spoke to Samson of all the fun he would have had being brought up in nature, surrounded by horses. As he nestled in his white box, we drove around our village, sharing with him the places we had hoped to see him grow up in, make friends, play, run free, and be loved. But his spirit was meant to rise back to the heights of freedom, roaming in the wonderland of heaven. So, we let him go home to fly free.

Our hearts ached. We were no longer who we had been, and there was no turning back.

It felt like losing control as I surrendered and merged with the grief, barely able to function or talk. Little did I know my life was on the precipice of a dramatic shift, a time that would often prompt the question, "Who am I? "

My horses knew. Donner has always possessed magnetism, with her graceful ways and striking looks. On this day, she caught my eye in a different way. As my emotions and feelings began to flow, I sensed something shift within me, again and again. My emotions bubbled to the surface, as if something fluid, formless, and ever-changing had come alive inside me.

Donner held my gaze. Her powerful focus would not be denied as the energetic communication began between us. She opened my heart to display what lay within, making it hard to breathe or think. Together, we listened to the melodies my heart sang.

The teaching began when her equine body language displayed all the traits of my personality and the chaos of my life. I watched her with fresh eyes. She mimicked my fast, shallow breathing and tense facial expressions by stamping her legs in frustration and tensing her sleek body.

With sheer majesty, this horse became a symbol of why I wasn't moving forward.

She was ME! She was mirroring my behavior with her body language. I cried as she drew me further into her caring heart. My rush of shame and guilt dissipated as she gently soothed and accepted me. There was no judgment from her—no blaming, no should or should not. She simply altered her breathing pattern and began taking deeper, slower breaths, in and out.

I followed her lead and regulated my breathing to match hers. Breathe, just breathe. Calmness descended. Donner had triggered my relaxation response. My face softened and my body and mind became still. She embraced and nurtured me in the same way she would comfort one of her herd. Her healing was without punishment or force, with no judgment of good or bad. All I needed to swim in the luxury she so generously offered was pure acceptance of everything that was, as I drew the innermost parts of myself to the surface for a non-judgmental examination.

Allowing a majestic creature of Earth to lead me back to my roots was the most natural and nourishing experience of my life. I began to recognize my automatic response to the world around me by watching Donner's behavior.

A horse was teaching me how to create a peaceful life.

Peace could only be found when I let go of the past and future and became grounded in the moment with her. This is how the herd lives. By observing the horses, I recognized that being released from the cage of life allowed me to witness the present moment and then become present in the moment myself.

My horse's shield of protective energy had allowed me to witness what felt like a timeless place. As I awoke each morning after that, my outer, physical world grew increasingly silent, and my inner commune with the herd blossomed. I experienced true love.

Experiencing this spellbinding wonder with my beloved horses, during a time of terrible grief, was only possible because of our deepening, heart-to-heart connection. Donner, the horse I have always described as "love," was the first to show me the inner workings of the outer world I was creating. She is blessed with such beauty and wisdom that it has been easy to let her teach me how to create a new and more fulfilling life.

To this day, Donner's behavior and expressions mirror my emotions.

Grief had stopped me in my tracks and made me aware of my feelings. I had seen my own behavior reflected to me through Donner's equine actions.

As I sat and listened, my heart had ached more deeply, not only for myself but for the previous generations. Driven by relentless fear, they had created the chasm that separates, divides, and dissolves our unity and love.

This stoic and humble but magnificent horse showed me with such generosity and honesty that our suffering is unnecessary! Yes, pain is symptomatic of trauma, but our sadness is part of our pursuit of that everlasting goal from which gladness can also arise, bringing with it the promise of peace on which hope rides.

In my despair, I couldn't logically understand all the pain I felt. The horses drew from me deep-seated, hidden sadness and discomfort. They displayed their natural ability to define a hidden attribute and to seize it and pull it to the surface for examination.

To me, it felt like the most magical untying of a complex web that was intricately knotted with emotions, all of which had been triggering patterns of behavior.

The horses understood me from the inside out, somehow better than I knew myself. How could this be?

I realized that life was going to be very different from that day forward.

Our horse-and-owner relationship had changed at such a deep level that it required justifying everything I had done with them in the past. Seeing into their souls and witnessing the beauty was more than intriguing—it was life-changing. Everything had turned inward. My life was not what I'd thought it to be. The herd left me humbled beyond words. They recognized how badly my soul within suffered to be free from limiting emotions.

The horses saw who I was, and I witnessed myself in their reflection. My yearning for freedom was a dark illusion. Yet, in an instant, they showed me how to view the physical world from my growing awareness. As my perspectives altered and expanded, I recognized I *was* free. We are all free. We just can't acknowledge it because of the linear mind-set we were taught.

The horses spoke of the wisdom we hold. It never dissipates or disappears; we just forget it's there. My resistance fell away as I became embedded in the knowledge of being. Everything we search for is hidden right here in existence. Expecting life to remain blissfully simple, I swam in the ocean of understanding. However, most who follow this path soon discover they cannot keep this secret to themselves, and their lives naturally bend toward service to others.

My life took new twists and turns.

Unable to fully articulate my new understanding, I attracted challenge after challenge until I learned how to own my voice and speak my truth. This has been excruciatingly difficult. I had thoroughly chained, boxed, and compartmentalized my denial of who I was.

The freedom of expression between me and the horses was natural. Gently, they eased me into my new way of being. But their behavior was a stark contrast to the response I received from people.

Many misunderstood my message. But there was no going back now, no matter how unpleasant these situations were. I had detached from the ritualistic patterns of relationships and refused to be labeled or defined by what I did or didn't do for someone. And I could not bear to identify with any drama or game that was being played out.

My experience of unconditional acceptance and love from the horses was the purest and most freeing way to serve.

Instead of hearing gossip and drama, I listened to my awakened inner voice. The pulse of my soul was drawing me forward, past fear, as I clasped the hand of love to ride upon the wave of freedom. Each new opportunity removed a link from the chain that had once tightly bound me. With each new lesson learned, my strength grew and the love I had to share began to shine. I could see it reflected to me in the mirror of my horse.

Donner's powerful gaze beckoned for a deeper fire to rise. We held what can be described as communion: a powerful exchange of knowledge and wisdom.

With each passing day, the horses relaxed into a deeper state of contentment. A peaceful calm descended upon the herd. They, too, were experiencing growth from our deepening connection. Their wistful looks, subtle gestures, and inner and outer communication never went unnoticed.

Their wisdom and understanding of the workings of life, energy, and consciousness soon became more obvious. Like us, like all creatures, they have a purpose here on Earth. Their lives are precious, sacred, and meaningful. They have told me many times that we are all one and that their intention is to help us fly home as one flock.

Animals gently try to direct us back to who we are and to our true nature, our true essence. They can assist in our search if we let them. Holding their gaze for one second longer can sweep away a lifetime of troubles.

They teach us love never denies us, controls us, or prohibits our movements. Love is free flowing. It allows mistakes and never judges or refutes our efforts, because we are love. Creatures are love in its perfect form. They know we share love, collectively and equally. They are shouting to us to come and claim what is rightfully ours and to let go of the fear we hold.

I believe the animal kingdom knows what the future holds for mankind.

Their knowing is innate. They don't have doubts, like humans do. When we can observe animals from a place of being without judgment, we will be able to access the deeper parts of our own consciousness, which will assist us in the growing shift from attachment to detachment and from division to unity.

Becoming whole can be extremely challenging. Unlearning all we have learned can prompt huge resistance in our bodies and psyches. But when you trust a life born without a physical voice, and listen with your heart, there is no distortion in the truth you hear.

You see, animals will never lie to you, and neither will nature. If you listen to their whispers, the inner spark patiently waiting to reunite all life will awaken. A dance begins within you, exciting you in a way that feels familiar and causes life to suddenly take on a beautiful and extraordinary glow. From out of nowhere, you appear, planted in a whole new Earth beating with vibrancy and love—an Earth where miracles do happen, and all life can reside harmoniously together.

The day my son Samson rose high to the heavens, to become one with the creator, I thought I had lost everything. In retrospect, that was when I gained everything. He did what he set out to do: He reminded me to listen to my heart.

The memory of his lifeless, tiny hand lying on his perfect heart is imprinted upon me for life. There is no greater reminder of the message he came to share.

Samson knew I needed help, and he recruited the most amazing teachers. Had I not listened to what the horses were trying to convey, my life would be without the color and vibrancy it now holds. Horses gave me the ability to embrace friendships, relationships, and experiences with a new perspective, to ensure freedom and purity is upheld for all through unconditional love, actions, and words.

The horses know that, to free the world of conditions, we must first free ourselves. They also know we have to experience life before it can become our truth, which then enables us to love this truth and share it.

As my love Samson showed: "Listen to your heart."

Danny's Story:
His Wind Beneath My Wings
by Gina Roda

Loving myself is the most important change and mission in my life.

As I crawled into bed, I prayed with fervor for a clear understanding of my life purpose. I prayed for healing in my life, including my relationship with Danny. We had not spoken for the six weeks since our break-up. But I missed him and was afraid we would never see each other again. Confused, I needed an answer from God!

Danny, my beloved, was a study in light and dark. He was a brave Spirit Warrior, both fearless and careless. He deserved to be loved and nurtured, but until me, he never had been! Danny and his six siblings had grown up in Benson, Arizona. His impoverished Apache/Yaqui/Mayan family lived in the shadow of the trucks rumbling down a freeway that sliced through the desert. Danny had dreamed of becoming a trucker and owning a truck; when he finally accomplished that, he felt he had found the last piece of the puzzle.

His life was chaos, drama, and trauma.

Danny had lived a wild life of tragedy and addiction. He spent time in prison after shooting a drug dealer in the kneecaps. His sixteen-year-old son drowned in a lake, and Danny never recovered from the loss. His first wife committed suicide at the age of thirty-three. His daughter was kidnapped and sold to people he didn't know, and he didn't find her again until she turned thirty-six. He had a tortured heart, but he deeply loved his family.

His first words to me were, "I know you're the woman who will tame my soul." My soul would never be the same after that.

Now, I only wanted to hold him close to my heart, hear his voice express unconditional love, and say our nightly prayers together.

At 2:35 a.m., I prayed, "Heavenly Father, Thy kingdom come, Thy will be done. Please guide me. If I am supposed to be with Danny, show me in a way that I understand—and if he is not for my highest good, please remove him from my life in a way I understand." I drifted into a troubled sleep about two hours later.

The next morning, I awoke with a heavy feeling.

It was as if I had traveled through the Dark Night of the Soul during the night. Something felt seriously wrong. I sought a healing from a friend, hoping she could help me balance my spinning energies.

The phone was ringing when I returned home. It was my dear friend Annette, a Yaqui medicine woman who was also a good friend of Danny's family.

"Gina, did you receive my message?"

"No, what message?" I asked.

"I'm sorry to tell you this. Danny died early this morning, at about 2:45 a.m. He was killed in a hit-and-run on the freeway."

My heart stopped. I couldn't catch my breath. The life I had known shattered into a thousand pieces as I listened in disbelief. This was my worst nightmare! Why would Danny choose to leave in this way?

Annette said, "He was called out for a late-night tow, helping young teens who were stalled and drunk on the side of the freeway. A trucker hit him as he was walking in front of his vehicle."

The details were too painful, too devastating, but she continued. "They believe he was killed instantly. The truck driver left him splattered across the freeway and never looked back or tried to help him."

My mind screamed, *No! No! No! He never said goodbye or made peace with me.*

"Because it was a hit-and-run, the accident is under investigation. His body was taken to Tucson for an autopsy. There's no way to see him."

I hung up the phone and sobbed. Then, I suddenly realized he had died about fifteen minutes after my prayer. What had I called forth? Was my prayer answered in this terrible way, or was it just his time?

The agony in my heart was unbearable. My soul was shaking.

The night of Danny's birthday, our relationship had seemed to be spiraling down. We'd both felt a sense of separateness and uncertainty.

His birthday night had been a disaster, as his past mistakes flashed before him. His eighteen-year-old son Juan had confessed to him that night how much he had suffered through his childhood with feelings of abandonment, pain, anger, and explosive hatred.

I could only listen quietly and let them speak their hearts. The dark shadow of their past had clouded the birthday celebration. It had also started the timer on a ticking bomb.

A few days later, Danny had called me, so excited. "Honey, oh my God, I have good news! I had a very deep dream this morning. My dead wife came to me. We were flying in Heaven together, so free and happy. She showed me her whole life, all the times we spent with our son Juan. She asked me to take him back to those places we spent time together when he was a baby, so he could see her life from the beginning. Honey … she came for me."

I'd felt a wave of nausea and dread. Danny was leaving.

Frantically, I had asked him to delay the trip. "Juan's going to graduate in a few weeks, and I'm scheduled for major dental surgery in May. I'll need your help. Can you just wait 'til June 4?" I'd pleaded.

Later, I would understand why I'd chosen that date. Through coincidence or divine intervention, Danny died in the early morning hours of June 4.

As planned, he had picked me up in Tucson that Sunday afternoon. On the journey back to Benson, we saw a huge diamondback rattlesnake crossing the road. Danny had jumped out of the car to offer his respect to the creature, while I watched from a safe distance. We'd arrived at Danny's apartment twenty minutes later. Feeling dizzy, I'd called Annette, the Yaqui medicine woman, to ask her to do a healing on me.

"I can't come now," she had replied. "Danny's parents had rattlesnakes get into their house through the holes in their walls. As I was running out to help them, I saw four rattlesnakes in my front yard. My husband pulled me back and said, 'You're not going anywhere. This is a serious message. It's not good!'"

The universe seemed to be speaking in symbols again. Seeing rattlesnakes is considered a bad sign in many cultures. In our culture, it means possible danger, death, and darkness.

As that night progressed, I had felt surrounded by intense, dark energy. Danny had gotten up early and avoided me. We'd exchanged some unkind words. Then I'd packed all my things, saying, "I'm leaving after my dental appointment. I'm not comfortable being with you."

He had driven me home from the appointment. As he stood in my kitchen, I'd walked past him and said, "See you later."

That was the last time I saw or spoke to my beloved Daniel.

I had thought that he would call, as he always did, and say, "Honey, I'm sorry."

But weeks went by in silence. Nightly messages in my dreams urged me to call him, to reach out to him, but something always stopped me. Was it pride, or was I being divinely protected? Was this the beginning of the change?

To see if reconciliation was in our future, I'd called my astrologer. "Danny's going to have an issue on June 4," Bibi had said. "He has a death T-square." That's a sign of death in astrology.

After Danny's funeral, I looked back at the reading and all the other synchronicities. The astrologer had mentioned the exact date of his death, June 4, but I hadn't wanted to believe it. I'd planned to spend my life with him. I called it the Danny Man Plan: Danny for the rest of my life.

The many lessons were blessings in disguise.

When did the changes start, and why did they start? I reflected on our three years together and saw I had been codependent, living my life just to be with Danny. Now, I am fully living my purpose, and writing is the most significant piece of it. As I honor Danny's life, I am celebrating mine and the gift of more time on Earth to grow, expand, explore, learn, and love.

Loving myself is my most important mission. I've learned to be unattached, to let go of all control and stay present to the heart of God within. I've found a way to love myself unconditionally and to value and cherish myself, even without Danny's love.

Danny's death helped me go deeper into my spiritual practice, with more prayer and inner-child work. I learned to find peace during the dark storms and to be less attached and needy. Love, no matter how fleeting, can change your life.

Danny had said, "I love every single thing about you. You don't have to change anything for me"—and he'd meant it. He was my fire power, and I was his wind power; I was the wind beneath his wings. He was my Man Plan, and nothing else had really mattered—or at least, that's what I'd believed at the time. I now know, years later, that God had a bigger plan for me that did not include Danny. *Thy will be done.*

Danny still comes to me in dreams and says, "Please be happy. Find someone else. I want you to be taken care of. I'll always be there watching over you. You were my healing angel."

We were each other's healing angels.

Danny's life and death inspired my soul. Although he did not consider himself a hero in his life, he died being a hero to others. It's my honor and privilege to acknowledge his goodness.

His death sparked a necessary change that allowed me to connect with an aspect of myself I had not noticed before. Danny was a perfect mirror reflection of me: light and dark, faith and fear, consciousness and unconsciousness. It had been challenging for me to look at my issues around relationships, but he was the catalyst for my most significant and profound emotional change and healing work.

Now, the change is complete. The circle of love is unbroken. Universe says it's time to turn the page to another chapter in my infinite book, which I've discovered is my life purpose.

The Loss
By J.S. Drake

We never know who just might need the light that we are.

How delicate our experience
Like the petals of a flower.
When storms ensue,
Uprooting our beloveds …
Leaving us
Crushed.
Broken.
Ripped wide open.
When we lose the Light of our Lives …
Why does the sun still rise?

excerpt from *May I Only Leave Rose Petals*
by J.S. Drake

It started just like any ordinary school morning, as my phone alarm yanked me out of my deep slumber and into the still darkness of the room. Groaning, I slowly willed myself to crawl out of bed and take a shower to start my day. There was no way to know this would be the day my world would crash down on top of me.

At about 7:30 a.m., I heard the sirens.

As my sister and I hopped into my car, we prayed to protect whoever was in trouble. "God, please be with whoever may be hurt," I whispered. And with that small prayer, I turned the key and drove the short distance to our small, rural school.

When I walked into the school, I overheard a junior talking about my best friend Jesi being involved in a car accident. Worry and anxiety welled up inside me. Jesi and I had been friends since the beginning of fifth grade, and she was one of the most important people in my life.

To calm the panic steadily rising within me, I practically ran to find my sister—but before we could talk, the bell rang for the first period. In French class, I couldn't concentrate, overcome with fear that Jesi had been hurt. It never occurred to me that she might have died. That didn't seem possible. My plan was to rush to the hospital and give Jes huge hugs and kisses, and then chew her out for scaring me. She'd smile and say, "You, silly goose, what are you talking about?"

About halfway through first period, my rising anxiety became too much to bear. I asked my French teacher for permission to call my mom, and soon, Mom was on her way to pick up my sister and me.

The brief car ride home, with my brother in the front seat and my sister and me in the back, felt eerily quiet. The sensation was like being in a slow-motion movie scene, watching myself. I was genuinely surprised to see we were heading toward our house instead of the hospital. *What in the world is going on? Why aren't we going to see Jes?*

"Mom, what are we doing?" I finally managed to croak out.

"Let's just go inside," she said.

By this point, I knew something was terribly wrong, and my heart sank to my knees as I fought against letting the terror overwhelm me. I remained calm. Inside the house, my sis and I stood close to one another and waited for my mom to say something, *anything…*

She looked overcome with anguish and quietly said, "Jesi died in the—"

Unable and unwilling to believe what I was hearing, I began to shout, trying to shut out the harsh reality of my mom's words, which seemed heavy enough to crush me.

"What? No, you're lying, Mom!"

"No, honey. Jesi didn't make it—"

"NO! NO! NO!"

The primordial gush of emotion that erupted from the depths of my shattered heart and soul could no longer be contained.

Those screams couldn't be mine, could they? But they were. I howled in anguish and agony, sinking to the floor. My mom wrapped both my sister and me in a fierce embrace, trying to hold our world together, but it was too late. How could a mother kiss or hug away this amount of pain?

I seemed to be standing outside of myself, looking down on this heart-breaking turmoil while also trying desperately not to drown. *How could this happen? And why? Why Jesi?* Why the vibrant, young, beautiful, and funny redhead who was my best friend? Why the girl who had brought so much love and kindness to the world?

"God, not Jes, please not Jes," I wailed for what seemed like forever, while in the fierce embrace of my mom and sister. I felt like there was no longer a reason to live.

Time seemed to be both speeding and crawling by, at the same time.

My mom asked us if we wanted to be back at school, where everyone else was receiving the news. We did. Seeing everyone crying in the halls, hugging and supporting one another, brought my tears back. Jesi's family was there, in shock, consumed by grief and numbness. Nothing I could do would console them.

Returning home later that day, my once-cheery house seemed dark and bleak.

Today, thirteen years later, Jesi will forever be sixteen.

Where would we be today, if she were still alive? Who would she be? Who would I be? I'll never know. But what I can say is this: Jesi was exceptionally kind. She had been the first to reach out to me in the middle of fourth grade, when I was reeling from my parents' divorce. More significantly, when I'd felt bullied and shunned, she had been my affirming love and light. She'd made me feel that I was a worthy person to know.

Her loss set in motion a period of illusion, despair, and many dark nights of the soul for me. I'd often wonder, "Why is the sun shining and the sky so blue? Shouldn't the whole world be mourning the loss of this beautiful soul?"

I came to realize that these circumstances of loss make us who we are.

Now I feel grateful for the gift of Jesi's deep friendship, which taught me the power of connecting with others from the heart and helped me develop the strength to share my life experiences.

The truth is, Jesi is still here with me, influencing and blessing my life. Her message to the world was simple: Be kind to others. My mission now is to choose to be kind, every chance I get—especially when others are not. That's the legacy she left. All the lives she touched through her compassion still ripple out and continue to touch more lives, in a never-ending blessing and testimony to the love she embodied.

When we lose the light of our lives, why does the sun still rise? I have the answer now. It's because, no matter what, we are all connected. The sun coming up is a reminder that—even in the depths of our pain, when we feel surrounded by darkness—we are a part of a community.

The sun, our collective light, shines in our darkest hour and reminds us of the light that we are.

The Revealing Nature of Grief
by Jane Anderson

Volumes of quotes have been written, spoken, and posted about NO REGRETS. Well, I have plenty!

The frantic voice of my daughter's roommate rocked me to my core. It seemed nearly impossible to decipher her hysteria. Finally, I understood the words.

"Tammie died. Jane, I found … I just found her … in her bed. When she didn't answer her phone … I just found her. She's dead. I don't know what to do now."

In that instant, every bit of air was sucked from my lungs.

How could this be true? Tammie would be coming home for Thanksgiving in four weeks. We would visit family and enjoy a big dinner together. High on the priority list was to take a current photo of us all together, at home.

Now, in a heartbeat, my plans melted away under the weight of a new reality. My first-born daughter, age thirty-eight, was never going to come home. I would never even hear her voice again. My plans would be forever changed.

The call had come during a Tuesday night meeting of our ladies' Bible study.

If you ever receive devastating news, the best place to be is with heart-sisters studying the word of God together. Somehow, I found the strength to tell them, "It's my daughter's roommate. My daughter died."

These words couldn't be coming from me! They sounded like the forced whisper of a stranger standing behind me. But in an instant, every woman in the room surrounded me. They descended like angels, covering my raw emotion and soothing every hurt. These beautiful women became the first of many to comfort our family through the weeks to come.

In stressful situations, especially in death, even the best of friends can struggle for the right words to express. Words escape us. Our vocabulary disappears when we need it most. I learned through this experience that there is no right or wrong way to convey sympathy and no perfect phrase that pacifies the deepest heartache. But when your heart is bursting with genuine compassion, your voice will speak peace to the hearts of the hurting.

Even weeks later, Tammie's death didn't seem real to me. I replayed, over and over, the times she'd called me "just to talk." Her first words had always been, "Hi, Mom, I just wanted to hear your voice today."

Tammie was knowledgeable. She often called when she came across something she thought I should know—whether I wanted to know it or not. Politically savvy, she kept me informed of the latest news, ignoring my extreme disinterest in politics. Tammie would rattle off sports statistics, even knowing I am barely able to match a logo or jersey colors to a team.

With our polarized interests, our minds were obviously wired in opposite patterns. Sometimes we argued. It still hurts me to recall the silly things that became conflicts between us. Now I can see how trivial those things were. They didn't matter.

I've had many conversations with God asking—no, begging—Him, "Please tell Tammie I'm sorry I didn't listen better when she called me. I should have been more present in the conversation. Please let her know I didn't mean the arguments we had when we didn't agree on things that really had no significance. And God ... please tell Tammie that I should have been more empathetic toward her. I'm so sorry."

Sometimes, Tammie called to tell me about something funny that had happened. Other times, she wanted to pour out her sense of sadness or defeat because her life wasn't turning out as she had hoped. She had asked me so many times to pray for her to find a husband, so she could have a family. I couldn't understand then why God wouldn't grant the desires of her heart. But God's plan included something different. At age twenty-one, Tammie would have a spinal tumor. At age twenty-five, she would develop MS—and at age thirty-eight, her body would shut down.

Do I have regrets?

Volumes of quotes have been written, spoken, and posted about NO REGRETS. Well, I have plenty! But I'm working on having fewer of them by following hard after God—by choosing to run to Him and strive for Him instead of striving for material things that don't matter.

After eight years of silence, I've decided to share this story about what it means to lose a daughter, because I know that someone has lost a loved one or is in the process of coming to terms with this kind of loss. There can be no instant healing from the type of change loss brings. There is no magic formula for dealing with the traumas we encounter in this life.

It isn't always easy to consider how our words or actions will write our future. It's challenging to take the long view and create memories—the things we want to remember—from our present moments. It's not always clear what each next right step should be.

Those of you who know me will recognize my mantras, some of which are:

"Mind your moments, because they become your memories."

"Live grateful. Be thankful."

"Bitter or better—I choose."

"Always look for joy."

I pray that these mantras might begin guiding you into a life of fewer regrets. We must cherish our moments and be present, right where we are.

Please remember this: Be attentive when you are the audience. Just forgive whatever might be destroying your happy ending—because it's not worth it. Hug often. Call and say you just want to hear their voice.

And always remember to say, "I love you."

The Day I Lost My Beloved Companion
by Ellie Pechet, M.Ed

She said she is going to come back to me in my
next life as a close and loving relative.

I searched the whole enclosed area, looking frantically under the places she tended to wedge herself—but she was nowhere to be found. Gone!

I hunted for her on the steps and inside the house. No Ellie Jr! Fear gripped me. Might she have wandered into the dense woods behind the house?

Thus, began my frenzied, eight-week quest to find my shell-baby, who had been an important family member for more than thirty years. Eventually, my grief began manifesting, without my knowledge, into a painful health condition.

I had shared my dream about a tiny turtle with a friend.

The next day, she showed up with a gift for me: a turtle. "What am I going to do with this?" I asked. She shrugged. Her gift had been a sweet gesture, so I accepted this little dream turtle. The length of her nails and the shape of her shell proved the turtle was female. I named her after me—Ellie Jr.

Ellie Jr.'s first home was a fifteen-gallon tank, perfect for her small size. One summer day, as a friend was helping me clean her tank, it shattered. We bought her a fifty-gallon replacement tank that afternoon from the closest pet store. Looking back, the tank accident might have been Ellie Jr.'s way of letting me know she wanted to move to a more spacious home.

Breaking down the enormous, new tank was hard work, but her happiness and health were more important to me, so I faithfully cleaned that big tank every month for thirty-five years.

One of my favorite things to do was sit on a chair right in front of the tank and press my mouth against the glass. Ellie Jr. would put her beak in the same spot, and we would linger that way, exchanging kisses through the glass. I often gave her Reiki energy healings, and when she was on her basking platform, I would gently run my fingertips down the top of her bony shell.

When Ellie Jr. had eaten her fill of smelt fish, I'd hold her in my hand and slowly stroke the front of her shell, giving her a shell massage—yes, a turtle shell massage! My fingertips would put her into a trance. Her flippers would wag back and forth, and her head would loll to one side. After a few minutes, I'd tuck her back into her tank where she'd remain in a hypnotized state, hunkering under the water.

This special turtle taught me so much about reptiles, and love.

In the summer of 2018, Ellie Jr, my two old cats—Blue and Snickers—and I were living in the mountains of North Carolina. The house was along a dirt road full of ruts, far off the beaten path. Ellie Jr. often let me know she wanted to walk around the house. I think she wanted to feel more included with me and the cats. She even liked to sit on my bed.

One Sunday in late June, she seemed especially eager to climb out of her tank. Although I was preparing for a phone meeting, I grabbed her from her tank and set her down on the bedroom carpet.

Animals understand what we say, and I asked her, telepathically, not to go under the bed. She usually stayed within view. But when I returned to the room a short time later, she had disappeared. I discovered her far out of reach under my California King-size bed! I had to use a "grabber"—the kind of device older people use to pick up things they can't reach—to pull her out from her cozy hiding place.

My energy was not smooth because I was stressed, and she didn't like the way I handled her.

I wasn't angry, but my energy must have seemed impatient when I carried her outside and set her down in the fenced-in area I'd created for her and the cats. Ellie Jr. headed for the other side of the pen. When I came out after the phone call, I didn't see her anymore.

I searched everywhere. After Ellie Jr. had been missing for two to three weeks, torrential downpours began, pelting the ground with more rain than I had ever experienced. It became an even darker time of frantic worry and also reflection. Intuition told me she was upset and teaching me a lesson by staying away. I couldn't blame her. I'd allowed my irritation and stress to overtake my respect for this wonderful, sentient being. Devastating guilt and remorse consumed me. I had been responsible for her welfare, and now she had vanished—and the nearby woods were filled with predators.

Beside myself with worry as the days and then weeks passed, I called two animal communicators to see if they could determine her location, without success. Containers of water and bits of the smelt fish she loved failed to draw her back home. I did everything I could think of to find her.

In desperation, I called a search-and-rescue dog handler.

As we combed through the woods near a small brook, one of her dogs picked up Ellie Jr.'s scent! The turtle must have been sitting on the bank and slipped into the fast-flowing current.

An acquaintance familiar with the area told me the brook flowed into the only pond on the mountain, several miles downstream. Could my beloved turtle companion be there? We met at her house and walked to the pond, dragging folding chairs to set them up on the bank. Hoping to see Ellie Jr., I focused on a corner of the pond filled with lily pads.

Within thirty seconds, Ellie Jr. popped her little head up, blinked, and looked right at me. I was shocked! We watched each other for just a moment before she sank back under the water and disappeared again.

A few weeks later, I returned to the pond, hoping to have another connection with Ellie Jr.—even if only one final time, because I was getting ready to relocate to a new area. I sat for more than an hour trying to lure her with the scent of smelts but did not see her again. I left heart broken.

The next day, I woke up with a rash on my upper back.

At first, I thought I must have brushed against poison ivy at the pond. The rash worsened, and painful welts spread to the side of my left breast and upper back. It became agonizing to sleep on my left side. A doctor at the clinic diagnosed shingles. The outbreak lasted for almost three months, because I was emotionally attached to my grief.

Later, Ellie Jr. communicated her story to me.

She had been trying to teach me a lesson the day she left. She hadn't planned to stay away, but she'd started to enjoy her adventure outside the fence. Then the rains had come, and she'd slipped into the swollen creek and was swept away.

She let me know how frightening it had been. She'd pulled her head and feet into her shell and flowed downstream until she landed in the pond, several miles away. That had begun the next chapter of what turned into an amazing new life experience as a wild turtle. As much as she loved me and didn't want me to be sad, she longed to live the rest of her life in the pond.

She said she had encountered four other native turtles, including a male who had befriended her and was teaching her how to live in a natural setting. The other turtles showed her what to eat, including minnows, fish eggs on top of the water, insect larvae, and certain grasses. She learned to hide in the tall grasses along the sides of the pond and she loved being able to paddle to her heart's content and then bask in the natural sunlight on the bank.

My beloved companion of thirty-five years let me know that she loved her new life. I was relieved that she seemed happy. I'm grateful to Ellie Jr. for the profound lessons she taught me about letting go. She made me realize, more than ever before, that all animals are sentient beings.

Although I miss Ellie Jr., I accept that she has been blessed with this new and ideal life as a wild turtle.

We still communicate telepathically now and then, and she has thanked me for the loving care she received for so long, and for letting her go to this next chapter in her life. She also said she is going to come back to me in my next life as a close and loving relative. Let the circle be unbroken.

Soul Story
by Deborah Beauvais

Each one of us has been given a gift and purpose.

That morning, just like any other morning, I said goodbye to my husband as he set off to work. A couple of hours later, the phone rang. A doctor at Norwood Hospital said the incomprehensible words: my husband had been killed in a motorcycle accident.

In an instant, our lives had forever changed. I got through the next days like a walking zombie as my daughters and I went through the motions of life.

My husband Rick was a special soul, a confidant, lover, friend, and the father of our three girls. He loved to read and instilled the same love within the girls by taking them to the library every week. After my tumultuous childhood and a first marriage filled with abuse, I was in awe of how sweet life could be with Rick. He was terrific in every sense of the word. Everyone knew I was grateful every day we were married.

My girls were twelve, thirteen, and sixteen at the time of their father's death. That first year without Rick was shrouded in mental fog, and the second was worse, because we were all emerging from the haze. Every time an ambulance passed we would instantly burst into tears.

I did my best to take care of our girls, but emotionally, I couldn't be there for them. While my body was on autopilot, my thoughts were obsessed with how I could join my husband.

Suicide beckoned. It was too difficult to be here on Earth without Rick.

For a couple of years, I thought about the best way to end my life. Taking a lot of pills was my first suicide choice. My second choice was crashing the car when I was driving alone. But each time I began to seriously consider suicide, my thoughts would return to my girls—our girls. They needed a living parent.

Responsibility wasn't new for me, but I found playing the role of both mother and father to three young girls overwhelming. Fixing the things that broke around the house frustrated me. Yet, six months into my grief— during the upheaval of adjusting to life without Rick—I felt something new: an overwhelming desire to help others.

I was driven to be of service to people in need.

Although I was zombie-like and "out of it" most of the time, I could not shake this desire. It was 1987, before grief support for young widows was available. The elderly might find grief counseling, but for young women, such support was nonexistent. And so, without guidance, my heart prompted me to step into the void.

One of Rick's friends who knew about my past, with both childhood and marital abuse from my first marriage, suggested I volunteer at a shelter for battered women and children. Working with others did not change the grief, which was always there. But the time I spent with these women was the beginning of my healing journey. I continued volunteering there for five years, while I searched for a way to be at peace living without Rick.

Life continued as I dug deep to find inner strength.

Even though my job had been waiting for me after Rick's funeral, it was hard to look people in the eye—especially those who knew about our exceptional relationship. One former client shared with me that learning about my wonderful relationship had saved her marriage. I took solace in her message as I continued to search for my answers to "Why me? Why take my Rick?"

After five years, I felt I had completed my calling of service to women and I stopped volunteering. Helping those women had been perfect for healing my earlier personal experiences, and I had discovered so much about myself from the experience. It had filled me up with love.

Next, I tried banking and then healthcare executive sales. With hard, determined work in sales, I experienced success, including opportunities for travel that made my schedule more flexible.

One day, I was invited to host a radio show in Providence, R.I. After thinking about it for three days, I said yes. Then, a couple of years later, someone suggested, "Why not have your own radio network?" For some reason, the concept resonated with me and elicited an inner excitement, even though I had no idea what to do.

I created Dreamvisions 7 Radio Network, a holistic internet radio station. Despite the initial mistakes and losses, I kept learning. Our station was created out of love with a mission to serve others. Eleven years later, the station thrives. D7RN is a full, operating station equipped with all the technical bells and whistles so people can tune into our amazing radio shows twenty-four hours a day, from wherever they are, all over the world.

Looking back, I know I was being guided.

I'm grateful to have had the opportunity, through the years, to experience profound messages and visits from my deceased husband, Rick. After searching for answers through books, practitioners, and healing modalities, I've learned that all the answers to life are within me, waiting to be discovered.

It's possible to find peace and freedom from emotional pain. My loved ones, both dead and living, wanted me to reclaim joy and thrive in life.

Each one of us has been given a gift and a purpose. Once we discover what these things are, we can become conscious creators and entrepreneurs, serving others. As we resonate in gratitude, we receive more love and understanding.

I believe we are eternal, and each of us has work to do on Earth— which, when completed, allows us to return home, to Heaven. We learn so much about ourselves through tragedy. We find gratitude in the moments we had with our loved ones as well as appreciation for our gift of life on Earth.

Rick returned home ahead of me. Through losing him, I gained confidence, inner-strength, and the ability to accomplish all my desires. I learned that I was never alone, being guided every step of the way by unseen celestial forces. It only required quieting my mind so I could listen, shift my focus off my grief, and focus on the needs of others.

Through devastating experiences, one can rise up, change, and become a better person.

I am grateful for having had Rick as part of my life and for experiencing all the emotions life brings with it. The extreme highs of joy and depths of despair from the pain were blessings. Being truly in love is the most phenomenal feeling—but my experience of love included the ups and downs of life and death.

I'm so proud of our girls. They turned out to be amazing women, each with determination and kindness that comes from the heart, and from their dad. Of course, they still wish their father could be here to experience all their special occasions throughout the years, including the birth of their children, his grandchildren. From a higher perspective, the girls are on their own journey of healing and growing.

Looking back, I don't know how I survived losing my husband. I do know this: We must believe in ourselves and remember there is a Higher Source of guidance. We must trust in the process of life.

The Invocation from Equus
by Jess Campmans

On the other side of healing is infinite inspiration.

She blew onto the top of my head with the wisdom and authority of a shaman. My own deep inhale filled my nostrils with the sweet smell of horse. I relaxed even more into the hard ground, where I sat directly underneath her neck.

She dropped her head and drew me closer to her front legs, her muzzle gently coaxing the base of my skull to release its upright hold and drop itself into the bow of reverent prayer. She had catalyzed a deep catharsis through an inner journey that had just given me back a long-lost piece of my soul, retrieving it from the deep, unconscious memories of a childhood accident—a near-fatal head trauma I sustained while riding a horse.

Growing up on a farm, surrounded by nature and animals, I found solace immersed in their world.

It had always felt more magical, safe and natural; like I belonged there with the animals, and less so with humans. So much of my childhood and adolescent years were spent with my horses. Of my many memories with them, one remains a pivotal point in my life.

It happened around my eighth birthday during a horse ride with my dad. I have three memories of that day: becoming unseated as my horse jumped, the ambulance ride with wailing sirens, and an elevator ride surrounded by doctors.

That day was the beginning of a long road, full of struggle to reconnect with my spirit.

Many years later, I stood sobbing in a beautiful horse barn. I couldn't stop the flow of tears or the anger and heartbreaking grief that wracked my body. On the farm, the cycle of life and death was ever-present. But another foal born deformed? The count of horses that required me to follow through with ending their suffering seemed to be growing exponentially.

"Maybe I'm just not meant to have horses," I told my husband. "I can't take this emotional pain anymore. Too many of them are dying. Besides, they don't even like me. Every time I go to them, they want nothing to do with me!"

To be totally honest, I wasn't sure I wanted anything to do with the person looking back at me in the mirror, either. My life seemed to be figured out; I was happily married, living on a farm with my animals and raising a family of four kids. This was all I had ever dreamed of. But nothing about the way I felt about myself and my life reflected the fulfillment that should have naturally come with that dream.

I couldn't bear the thought of selling my horses, but it soon became apparent that while they were usually peaceful, they exhibited signs of fight-or-flight tension whenever I entered their space.

It seemed pointless to continue with the way things had been going.

We lived in the house where my husband had grown up, and my daughter's bedroom had been home to not just one, but two of my husband's brothers who had passed. My daughter had been waking up nightly in complete terror, complaining of something "really bad" in her room. I invited a Reiki Master to come and see what she could do.

As I stood in my daughter's bedroom, silent tears streamed down my face. The Reiki Master—holding a lit candle, charcoal, and smoldering sage—asked if I could feel the angels and spirit guides that surrounded us. Yes. That was it. These spirits were as real as anything else in my life. Hearing her announce their presence helped me begin to remember what I'd lost as an eight-year-old on that fateful day with my father.

My Reiki experience had unlocked long-forgotten memories of my head injury and helped me reconnect with my infinite soul. And it had another effect as well. It became easier for me to enter my horses' space. My new perspective on life was mirrored by the horses. They began to seek me out.

With their guidance, I practiced Reiki by placing my hands on those that were willing to participate. Their thoughts and feelings would come through to me. Their bodies and mine would involuntarily exhibit signs of release and relaxation. Spontaneous tears would often erupt from my wellspring of emotion. The horses would follow my catharsis with a yawn, which led to greater acknowledgement of each other's presence.

One day, a patient mare became my shaman, helping me find the final missing pieces to my memory in just this way.

A whole new world opened up. I was insatiable, wanting to digest everything I could find about energy healing and deepening my relationship with my horses.

Equine Facilitated Learning equaled Energy + Healing + Horses. This was my path!

The idea of helping humans heal with horses spoke to something deep inside me that could not be ignored. Elated, I signed up for a certification class that caught my eye. But that night, I couldn't shake a nagging feeling in the pit of my stomach. At midnight, I awoke with a pounding heart, in full panic. Sweating and nauseated, I ran to the computer.

Disturbing details of the program jumped out at me. My expensive training would be in another country, taking me away from home for months.

Just see, came a thought out of nowhere. *Just see!*

Having no idea what it meant, I googled EFL certifications near me and found a local program that was only one week long. I registered for those classes and felt my stomach settle. Years later, I heard negative feedback about the program I'd dropped. Thank goodness my intuition had steered me away.

With my certification in hand, I established Guided by Equus, named in honor of my greatest teachers. My horses stepped easily into their role in this healing work, showing up to share even more. They were docile with me now. However, I found it puzzling that one of my pregnant mares would always leave when I offered my "healing hands," staying a well-established distance away. Two weeks later, I discovered why.

Flat on her side as the day's first beams of sunlight streamed into the barn, the mare was in labor—and something was very wrong.

Most mares can deliver their foals easily, but when there is a problem, it often means the loss of one or both horses. This particular mare had bloodlines that I had been seeking for years. The vet suggested a C-section, but the nearest clinic was far away. My mare seemed to understand what the consequences of that trip would be to her and the foal inside. She began pushing until she prolapsed, pushing her intestines outside of her body, which is a death sentence for a horse. "I'm so sorry, Jess," the vet said.

Time was now of the essence. Together, we pulled out the limp foal's body. Stunned by losing my mare, I was not about to let this filly die, too. Two pairs of hands began CPR; soon, the newborn sucked in a shallow little breath.

I assessed the situation before me: a mess of a mare, an orphan foal, and it wasn't even 8 a.m. yet. But the tide of death had shifted. The filly was alive. We started the process of milking and collecting colostrum from the mare before it was too late.

She knew, I thought. *She knew as soon as the vet said we'd have to haul them that they both would die. She sacrificed her life for her daughter.*

This echoed round and round in my head and heart as I sat on the ground cradling the head of my dying mare. Her steady nickering to me slowly grew ever softer, ever quieter. Yet, somehow, I felt reassured. Her gentle communication gave me a feeling of hope, a knowing in my body that everything would be alright.

As I began to consider all the work that would be involved in bottle-raising the foal, I felt as if someone were watching me. I looked up to see the black sister of my now-departed mare, who stood with her own foal. She looked straight at me.

Would you accept her? I wondered silently. The mare's head bobbed slightly.

To be sure that she had heard me, I asked again, out loud. "Would you adopt Carmelita's filly?" Her head bobbed again, nodding. Annie, the black mare, graciously adopted little Karma, nursing both the newcomer and her own colt. I marveled at my set of twins that summer.

A blessing had come from the curse. An awakening had transpired on a soul level.

Living a life guided by Equus has taken me out of the depths of my own hell, discovering and recovering all that I had ever searched for. It has helped me weave together a life splintered by trauma and provided healing as well as inspiration. I've reclaimed my relationship to the Mother, the Divine Feminine energy that I had abandoned into unconsciousness around age eight. The horses have initiated a path that will lead me to what I am meant to be.

Messages from our soul come to us through symbols, synchronicity, and shared experiences. They are the pathways for the universe/God/ Spirit, enabling a soul perspective that transcends fear and separation. This knowledge does not make loss any easier, nor does it grant a bypass of the existential process. But it helps us understand that grief is just part of the circle. May the circle of life and death, love and learning, be unbroken.

No one escapes loss. Life's most difficult challenges and struggles can either destroy you or catalyze hope and healing. The horses helped me realize I was not alone. The times that had shattered me were part of my soul's journey into self-realization and self-actualization. I found faith when there was nothing else left, and faith gave me the courage to find healing.

And on the other side of healing waits infinite inspiration.

Final Thoughts

Grief is love. Without love, there is no grief. Death is a painful part of the circle of life, a coming of age—but as these true stories showed, love never dies. It's the bridge that can connect us with our deceased loved ones. It is often through the death of another that we come into our own and become more self-reliant. Death is a stern teacher and grief is a natural, emotionally adaptive process to death.[1]

Many of the authors pointed out something backed by current research:[2] shifting attention from despair to the needs of others and focusing on personal goals and relationships can help diminish the chaotic winds of death and bring forth clarity. The authors in this section found healing in the company of humans and animals, illustrating the complex layers of our universal connection to oneness with nature. This truth is also shared and beautifully summed up in the next section's stories about *Life Journey and Identity: The Long and Winding Road*.

PART 4

LIFE JOURNEY AND IDENTITY
The Long and Winding Road

There is nowhere you have been
that has not been worth going

I Hope You Dance
by Rev. Patricia Cagganello

Believe in miracles, because you are a miracle.

My breath quickened and a lightness began to enter my heart. I knew that I had just received a valuable gift as I sensed a strong, supportive presence around me.

You are worthy.

Believe in miracles, because you are a miracle.

These words renewed my hope in the future and gave me a glimpse of my self-worth—something I hadn't felt in a long time.

Feel the joy even before you figure it out, the angels had said.

I clearly had a lot of work to do before I could reclaim a sense of joy and peace in my life—but now I'd been given some direction and guidance to follow.

The angels had suggested something that took my breath away: They encouraged me to dance more, to reconnect with my soul through the joy of music.

The angels had said I "moved like a pretty little bird," and they strongly suggested I attend a dance workshop at a retreat center in a neighboring state. They wanted me to get rid of my fear of dancing.

Lose your ego and enjoy yourself, they had stressed.

This was unbelievable. Of all the things the angels were telling me, I couldn't believe that they were telling me to dance. Dance to reconnect with my soul and to find my joy. Many times in my life, I had wished that I could feel the joy I saw on other people's faces while I watched them dance—looks of pure abandon and bliss, as if the music moved through them and became their very lifeblood, nourishing their heart and soul.

I yearned to feel that freedom.

But one unforgettable night, deep scars were burned indelibly into my teenage psyche. As frenetic flashes of color from the strobe lights cut across the dance floor and the deafening reverberation of the bass pounded in my ears, I whirled around and was confronted with a pointed finger and merciless cackles from a nearby group of girls. Under the pulsating disco ball, I was left exposed and vulnerable. Even after the Hustle finally stopped being the only dance in town, my feelings of awkwardness and inadequacy lingered.

My angels knew this. They said, *when you find the courage to dance, you will carry that new sense of self-worth into other aspects of your life.* It sounded plausible. But they wanted me to dance! This was huge for me.

But I had felt so bad for so long, and the promise of feeling joy tantalized my every sense. I was willing to try almost anything to feel better—even if it meant summoning the courage to dance in front of others.

I checked out the web site of a nearby retreat center, half hoping they wouldn't offer anything for me. Sure enough, right under the site's bright-green banner, a special event was listed: a two-day workshop that used dance as a means to express and connect more deeply to your inner self. I stared at the computer screen for a long time, unsure of what to do.

This was a defining moment for me. The angels had given me specific instructions. If I trusted their guidance, then I needed to be serious about following it. What would I choose: Could I find the audacity to face my own "not good enough" feelings head-on, hoping it might make me feel better? Or would I rather stay in this safe, but sad, shell I'd built around myself, secure in my misery? My decision had been made when I'd turned on the computer. I signed up for the workshop that day.

Quickly, doubt didn't just creep in; it *poured* in.

I frantically shoved my misgivings back, not wanting to find one tiny reason not to go.

What are you thinking? The workshop is next week! How are you ever going to make arrangements for your kids, your pets, and your house by next week? and more pointedly, *why would you ever go to a dance workshop anyway? You can't dance!* My ego and my Spirit locked horns. My head and my heart were mercilessly batted back and forth.

But somehow, all of my arrangements for my responsibilities—my kids, my pets, and my house—effortlessly fell into place. It became apparent that I was meant to go.

My departure day soon arrived. I packed my bags with yoga pants, T-shirts, and headbands—and threw in a touch of resiliency and self-deprecation, for good measure. I kissed my girls good-bye and tossed my bags in the back of my old, gray Nissan.

As I settled comfortably in my seat, a strange tingling ran down my spine.

Could this be the beginning of positive feelings starting to return to my body?

The retreat center, a series of brick buildings nestled protectively in the bosom of a nearby mountain range, was two hours away. Driving through the rolling New England countryside made the time pass quickly. "Get the Party Started," a rocking song from my favorite artist, Pink, blasted from the stereo on repeat. The rhythm and upbeat lyrics helped loosen my inhibitions as I drummed my fingers on the steering wheel and twisted to the beat. As the sun neared its apex, my car crested a hill and a vista of trees and gently sloping hills came into view. I'd found my home for the next two days.

A sense of community greeted me as I drove down the long, winding driveway. The energy in the air shifted, as if sensations of peace and contentment were infused into this space. Time seemed to slow, and I noticed little things: the clanging of the screen door as it closed loudly behind a guest, a lone dandelion missed by the gardener in the neatly-tended flower garden, and a majestic canopy of trees shading a wooden bench that beckoned me to sit and rest. People walked out of the woods, wearing hiking boots and clutching water bottles. I made a mental note to find out about the property's hiking trails.

My emotions fluctuated between *What the heck am I doing here?* and *I never want to leave!* My father's words— "Chin up, and shoulders back!"— came to mind. His wisdom brought a smile to my lips and tenacity to my heart. I parked the car, grabbed my bags, and marched into the foyer to sign in.

Thirsty from my drive, I was delighted to see a large carafe of fruit-infused water had been set out to welcome guests. After two big cups of strawberry-lemon water, I was refreshed by the tangy sweetness and ready to start. I registered, dropped my bags in my room, and followed the directions down to the workshop.

My newfound sense of confidence quickly abated as I walked up to the workshop door. A six-foot wide, three-level wooden shoe rack stopped me cold.

Sneakers, sandals, and ballet flats in all sizes—some small enough to fit a tiny woman's feet, others large enough for a very tall man's, and in shades from white to black and all colors in between—were there on that rack. But these were not just random shoes to me. My breath caught as I realized these were the shoes of the people I was going to have to *dance* with!

Who are these people? I bet most of them are great dancers ... especially whoever owns these pretty red shoes. My fears taunted me once again. *Could any of them be as nervous as me?* I halfheartedly hoped, feeling intimately connected to the owners of the anonymous shoes left on this rack.

I looked down at my size-ten, worn-out, black flip-flops and sighed.

I hesitantly placed mine on the rack with theirs, berating myself for not wearing nicer shoes, said a quick prayer, and went in.

The spacious, rectangular room was lined on two sides with tall windows, rounded at the top, which invited sunlight to stream across the glistening hardwood floor, casting comforting warmth into the room. As my mind noted the room's beautiful characteristics, my heart knew I was really entering a room filled with possibilities: a breakthrough, a fresh start, and a new perspective were all whispers on the winds of promise here.

Expectant, smiling people sat on the hardwood floor, waiting to begin. My mind quickly estimated that there had to be at least a hundred fellow dancers, but I especially noted a group of three women sitting together, casually chatting. They seemed to be about my age, and I wondered if they were friends who came together or if they had only just met. *Maybe one of them wore the pretty red shoes on the rack outside. . .* I thought, feeling self-conscious that I didn't have anyone to talk to, and my confidence faltered again. Against a wall in the back of the room, I sat down and tried to assess the situation. As I glanced at the door, I gratefully realized that the place I chose to sit also gave me an easy escape if I changed my mind.

Before I could flee, a young woman stepped up to the front of the room. Dressed in black yoga pants and a white tank top, she looked to be in her late twenties. With a sincere smile, she tossed back her long, brown hair and threw her arms wide, welcoming us. I anxiously thought back to what my angels told me during my reading: *We will not lead you somewhere you are not supposed to go.* I made a conscious choice to stay and trust them.

"We're going to jump right in," said Deborah, our instructor. Her warmth and exuberance comforting me. "Since this is expressive dance, there is no right or wrong way. Simply let the music wash over you, caressing each part of you, and move your beautiful body in response. Do whatever feels good to you."

Slow, unfamiliar instrumental music filled the room, and we all stood, taking cues from each other, and began to dance. At first, we danced individually, and I lost myself, a wounded bird trying out her wings. I moved nervously on the outskirts of this large mass of people moving and swaying their bodies to the music.

It wasn't so bad. If I closed my eyes, which I did frequently at first, I did feel the music. When I raised my arms above my head, the music would flow into my fingertips, gliding down my body and into my very core. The soft melody caressed my hurt and broken heart.

We danced this way for some time. The music would change, but I kept my eyes closed, still the wounded bird on the outskirts, gingerly testing her wings. Occasionally, I snuck a peek at the others, to make sure my movements didn't look too different. Eventually, I started to feel secure that I could survive this workshop.

But then the rules changed.

Just closing my eyes and retreating into myself, dancing amongst—but really at a distance from the others would no longer be allowed. We were now asked to dance *through* the crowd, and to stop briefly and dance with different people for a moment or two before we moved on to someone else.

Now I'd have to make eye contact, to seek out others and dance with them. Expose, even for the briefest of moments, the part of myself that I didn't feel confident in . . . and never had. *If I look into their eyes, would I see the same cruel laughter in their eyes I saw all those years ago under the pulsating disco ball? Would I feel the same humiliation?*

I glanced back at the large exit door I had walked through just a few short hours before—the escape I had tucked neatly into my back pocket. Two choices lay before me. One, I could walk out that door, out of the room, and not do it. Not put myself and my wounded heart out there. I could simply leave. That choice scared me more than the dancing. I knew that if I did that, then I would be stuck, stuck in this horrible "not good enough" feeling that I had been living with.

The other choice was to dance, not with my eyes closed in my own safe, secure world but with others. The little self-worth I had left from my divorce was not going to be enough to get me through this. I thought of my angels, felt them—a beautiful collective of light just above me—and asked for their help.

You told me to do this, I reminded them. Please be with me now.

My breath quieted my beating heart, and I moved through the crowd. Clumsy at first, I didn't make direct eye contact with the first few people, staring instead just above their eyes and dancing quickly away from them, not allowing them to see me through my eyes—the doorway into my soul.

The other people around me were smiling, laughing even; they were enjoying this. I forced a smile onto my face, determined to feel some of the joy that I witnessed in the room—even if I had to fake it. As I began to smile at my partners, they smiled back. We connected first through our eyes, and then with each new person, I connected a little more through the movement of our bodies. I slowly became part of this vibrant sea of swaying people; my smile became less forced, coming more from my heart and less from my mind.

Eventually, the music stopped. The first day was over, and I was glad, relieved really, but less relieved than I thought was possible. People hugged around me, seemingly happy for the closeness that this exercise brought to our group. We naturally drifted in groups toward the door, to collect our shoes and head to dinner. I grinned inwardly as a petite, red-haired woman in my group slipped on the pretty red shoes I'd noticed that morning. Her name was Cheryl, and with an easy smile creating fine laugh lines around her mouth and a sparkle in her green eyes, those shoes suited her perfectly.

Dinner was delicious, and the conversation in my group was light and engaging. We shared our stories—where we lived, family, kids, and jobs— just enough to create a bond but not enough to reveal who we really were.

A Buddhist meditation that evening soothed and uplifted my heart. Physically, emotionally, and spiritually spent from the day, I fell into bed and woke early, refreshed and ready for what the day would bring.

The morning dance passed pleasantly. Now I could now look into the eyes of my partners and truly smile back at them. I even found myself picking up one of the brightly colored scarves that were provided as props, twirling it as I danced. *Who am I?* I laughed to myself.

Near the end of the workshop, my newfound sense of ease was tested again.

With a smile wider than I thought possible, Deborah explained that she had something very special in store for us. During the next exercise, we were not going to dance with a partner but *for* a partner.

What? My mind raced. *Did she say* for *a partner? Dance while someone is specifically watching me?*

"Everyone, please find a partner," she mercilessly went on. "You will each take turns dancing alone. The role of the partner is to simply *watch* you dance."

I froze. This was too much.

Despite the increased confidence I had felt in the past two days, this was more than I was ready to handle. This wasn't pushing my limits; it was knocking them down and trampling on them as I raced past. The door, my escape hatch, loomed larger now. Was now the time to pull it out of my back pocket and run like hell?

People were talking, looking for someone to partner with. I hesitantly lifted my eyes and found another set of eyes—with a familiar green sparkle— staring straight into mine. Cheryl smiled, and I smiled back; I had somehow silently agreed to be her partner.

You move like a pretty little bird, Patty, my angels again reminded me.

Please stay with me! I pleaded to my angels. *Help me to feel the music, to become the music. Allow me to experience the joy of the music, not only in my body, but in my soul.*

In that moment, I realized this was what dancing was really about: feeling the joy. Dance was a chance to reclaim that part of myself, that connection, I had denied for so long. My angels knew. Once I found the freedom to dance, I'd also have the freedom to reconnect to that lost part of myself.

After a few deep breaths, I cast a final plea in the angels' direction and stepped onto the dance floor. Hesitant at first, but only for a moment as determination filled my veins. The importance of this moment was not lost on me, and I wasn't prepared to let it slip by.

You move like a pretty little bird, my angels said again.

And I did. I danced. I swayed. I swirled around and around. I gratefully felt the music caress me, and as I reached my arms up to the angels, I felt their warm embrace. My angels were with me, watching me. I smiled.

When the music ended, I felt a wave of disappointment, because I wanted to dance more. My eyes met Cheryl's as I walked off the floor.

"I truly enjoyed watching you dance," she shared. "Are you a professional dancer?"

I laughed and shook my head. "No, I'm not a professional dancer," I assured her. "But I really did enjoy dancing just now."

The workshop ended. My heart was fuller and my mood lighter, and with contentment now also packed in my bags, I drove home.

Two days of dancing had shifted something inside of me. But it wasn't just the dancing; my Spirit knew it had been so much more. I'd spent two days finding the confidence to step out into a sea of people and let myself be seen.

For two days, I'd shrugged off my self-limiting beliefs and a suffocating sense of unworthiness. For two days, I'd trusted the path that connected me with my inner self, knowing I was safe and supported.

I'd experienced two days of the kind of joy you feel when you surrender all your defenses and realize that you are worthy of being loved—not for *what* you are, or for *who* you are, but simply *because you are*.

This story also appears in Patricia's book *God is in the Little Things: Messages from the Golden Angels*

Coming of Age Overnight
by Sara Gouveia

Say "yes" to the things that you believe are best for you.

My life changed completely after my parents' divorce.

At the time, I was fifteen years old, and growing up in Portugal. So much change was already happening at that age; a change of schools, important exams, changes in friendships and love relationships, hormonal imbalances, and questioning my purpose in the world, and so on… all part of being fifteen.

My parents and their divorce affected my perspective for many years to come.

My father is an extrovert, a humorous person, and I am very much like him. He is also someone who had a difficult education and was never allowed to pursue his dreams. Whatever idea he would have, he only dreamt about but never put any real effort or commitment behind it to make it happen. I believe this was out of fear; fear of not being good enough in himself and his talent.

Despite this, he was always ready to try new things, and he encouraged me to do the same. "Never say you don't like something without trying it first," he told me countless times while I was growing up.

My mother, on the other hand, was much more reserved and emotionally distant in her quest for perfection. She'd also had a difficult childhood, nurturing five younger siblings, helping her parents manage the farm, and studying in school. But Mom made things happen. She was committed, and she would marry her goals. Although I felt her absence while growing up, her sense of achievement influenced me.

I had been very attached to my father. After the divorce, our connection was gradually torn apart while my connection with my mother grew in a new direction. Mom and I had the weirdest relationship, more like roommates rather than immediate family. I am happy it doesn't feel like that anymore.

My parent's marriage and divorce also deeply affected my future love relationships.

At the beginning of a new relationship, I'd be my father: sweet, warm, and caring. But then I'd become my mother: obsessive, distant and cold. Over time, this pattern began to shape my life, and I was ignorant of it. In the meantime, now that my mom was more present in my life, my ability to work hard and achieve goals improved.

Several years and heartbreaks later, two people became important parts of my life. One was my teacher, and the other was my lover. Both taught me differently about new possibilities and perspectives of life, and they opened my eyes to a greater world bigger than my own bubble.

I also grew closer to a cousin who taught me many things about life. She is a wonderful woman, humble, loving, and strong. With support from these relationships and an open mind, I began to search for self-help and self-development mentors in books, audios, and videos.

The world felt different now that my eyes were wide open.

During this time, my career as a veterinarian was just budding. I was able to find a position in a small animal practice near my home. I didn't want to accept it because I always wanted to work overseas and broaden my knowledge in equine practice. However, my cousin pointed out some serious concerns about that plan. Ultimately, she persuaded me to accept the nearby job offer.

A year and a half later, I couldn't work there anymore. My work schedule was creating a huge imbalance between my personal and professional life. All my hours were consumed with work, work, work, leaving no time to visit family and friends, entertain a boyfriend, have a hobby, or enjoy anything fun.

I had no control over my life anymore.

Every day seemed to belong to clients and patients, until I felt like I wasn't myself anymore. I updated my LinkedIn account, and over the next five days, several veterinary recruitment companies from the United Kingdom contacted me to ask if I'd be interested in working in the UK. I easily and immediately said, "Yes!" My cousin agreed this time, because I now had the resources to travel abroad.

I accepted a mixed-role job in the countryside of South Yorkshire. It was the best decision I've ever made. So much has happened since I moved to the UK! I've met amazing and inspirational people whose ideas match mine, and that was very inspiring. I began bouldering, a form of rock-climbing that was new to me, and I practice yoga daily. My eating habits evolved, first to a plant-based diet and then to complete veganism. And I created a blog about my experience as a vet, hoping to help others interested in working with animals to reach their full potential in their personal and professional lives.

I keep finding inspiration and more projects to put into action.

I am so grateful for the many opportunities that have come to me by simply saying yes to them. It worked as a chain, where one opportunity had led to another. Despite what happened in my past, this attitude is now a part of me and what I've became. Without it, I would never have accomplished the things that make me proud of myself. I couldn't be happier!

This is the motto I follow now: *Say yes to the things that you believe are best for you.* It doesn't matter how terrifying they might feel. There is no reason to think twice about a choice after it has been made, because doubt can prevent us from achieving anything in life, other than fear.

Life is always unfolding in the best way possible for me if I just let it.

Time to Get Out
by Rev. Stephanie Red Feather, PhD

*In many ways, I had to surrender to my own psychic death
for my rebirth to happen. It was not a graceful surrender.*

It's time to get out, I declared to my first husband. "Time for whatever's next."

My decision to leave the Air Force after almost ten years wasn't born from a clear vision of what the next chapter in my life would be. There was no, "GET OUT!" shout from the universe. It was just a faint voice, whispering in my heart.

In hindsight, it's a small miracle that I even listened, as my heart had long been banished from the decision-making table in favor of practicality, logic, and all things left-brain.

As I laughingly tell people now, "It wasn't like 'Hey, I know what I want to do next. It's time to get out.' It was more like, 'It's time to get out ... oh s#&@! Now what?'"

As a lifelong empath and people-pleaser, I had no clue who I was or what I wanted, so my next career choice seemed rather random. It came down to this: my financial advisor said, "Hey Steph, you're good with people. Do you want to be a financial planner?"

I liken it to the first time someone of the opposite sex shows interest in you in grade school: "Oh, you like me? Okay, cool, I'll like you back." So, I said, "Sure I'll be a financial planner!" with about as much authentic passion as a teenager taking out the trash.

I thought my financial advisor's endorsement meant I would be successful in this field. At that time in my life, I could neither recognize nor distinguish what I wanted from what someone wanted *of* me or *for* me. My sense of self was practically non-existent, and my locus of identity was centered in anything and everything else *but* me. Pleasing outer authority had been my unconscious motivation, driving all actions and decisions.

But that system was about to implode.

For the next year, I endured three levels of interviews, socked away more than a thousand dollars each month, and studied for my series of exams to sell insurance and securities. I learned the company's tradecraft, practiced my "spiel," and set up my office. Then, with great excitement, waited for the clients and money to come flooding in.

It turns out I had no clue how to run a business, listen to my heart, or manage my expectations.

But, to be fair to me, the company taught us to apply a prescribed system, but they offered no real advice for anyone who wasn't wildly successful doing it exactly that way. It was almost as if they blamed you for not using the tools, they *didn't* give you.

I bought their fast-start model hook-line-and-sinker. It was formulaic and supposed to be "foolproof." Just do A, B, and C like they showed you, and you'll get X, Y, and Z in return. Not enough XYZ? Do ABC more, and harder.

Failure had never crossed my mind, so while I was terrified at the slow start, I remained in denial that I was failing.

Yes, I could have asked for help—if I'd known what to ask for.

Each agent was an independent contractor, but we all worked out of a common office and shared an onsite district agent who mentored us and oversaw our practices.

One day our district agent Jack, who knew I had been struggling for months, barged into my office and sank onto my couch and while making hand gestures as if he was trying to collapse a balloon said, "You know, Stephanie, I've been trying to mold, shape, and train you ... and you just keep popping back into Stephanie!"

If I'd had the guts, I would have said, "No f$%@ing s&%$! That's because I *am* Stephanie!"

Less than six months later, I quit and was flat... out ... lost. In the ensuing years, I worked as a home health aide, a jewelry store associate, a performer of odd jobs, an admissions officer for a career school, a chiropractic assistant, a curriculum coordinator for another career school, and more. My self-loathing grew in the process, as I judged myself harshly for this maddening and confusing employment schizophrenia.

After high school, I had gone straight into college on a four-year Air Force ROTC scholarship. Upon college graduation, I'd received my commission and went on active duty. As my older sister wisely pointed out, "You never had the 'figure-out-who-you-are and decide-what-you-want-to-do' experimentation period that most people experience in their late teens and early twenties."

She was right. I was navigating that phase in my early thirties, and it sucked.

The one "job decision" I'd made at age sixteen had sustained me for the next sixteen years. I'd known it was time to "get out"—but the transition from military structure to civilian life was challenging. I was like a wild animal kept in captivity since birth and then released into a sink-or-swim world where I didn't know how to behave or stay afloat.

One by one, my carefully laid plans disintegrated as I entered what I later recognized as my spiritual awakening. In the space of four years I lost $25,000 due to quitting my business "too soon," borrowed thousands against the cash value of my life insurance policy, used up all of my savings and investments, went through eight jobs, moved twice including to a new state and in with my in-laws for a spell, borrowed thousands from family, was fired from three jobs, was on unemployment two times, and had a huge purging of personal belongings.

By the time I exited this "spiritual crucible," almost five years later, nothing in my life was recognizable from when I had left the Air Force. I lived in a different house in a different city and state. My paycheck came from a different job. I was in a different relationship, drove a different car, and had different possessions. My financial status was completely altered.

And I had a changed perspective on life.

While I was in the spiritual crucible, it felt like everything I counted on as solid and predictable betrayed me. Everything I believed in was stripped away. With each "blow," it felt like I was being squeezed through smaller and smaller funnels, until my pulverized parts could be mashed through a fine-mesh sieve and finally liquefied. In many ways, I had to surrender to my own psychic death for my rebirth to happen. It was not a graceful surrender.

Traveling through this awakening was the hardest experience of my adult life—harder even than enduring my divorce and my father's death.

I had no coping tools, skills, or awareness of what was happening. I was without perspective and devoid of a personal compass to keep me pointed toward my true North.

A couple of poignant memories remain from this gut-wrenching period. They illustrate the sheer desperate frustration I felt.

In my early years, I'd relied heavily on oracle cards. One day, in the makeshift "private" living room my ex and I had created while living at his parents' house, I was drawing a multiple-card spread. None of the cards made sense to me. I wasn't very adept at listening to my intuition and extrapolating the meaning to apply to my circumstances. In a childlike tantrum, I hurled all the cards to the floor and shouted at God, "These don't make any sense! Just tell me what to do!"

The current owners of my former house in Illinois might get a kick (pun intended) out of the story behind two black smudge marks on the kitchen ceiling. One evening, I came home so frustrated and swirling in my victim stew, that I kicked off each shoe—one and then the other—with all the force I could possibly muster, cussing at God and screaming. Each shoe flew directly up to the ceiling and left a black smudge. I was waiting to hear a satisfying *thwack* as they hit the wall. I even secretly hoped they would break something. Nope. Each struck the ceiling with a quiet little thump.

Of course, I concluded that I couldn't even do anger "right." More fodder for my pity party. At least it became a good story to tell now.

In metallurgy, refining consists of purifying impure metal.

I recognize now that, during this stretch of years, I was being alchemically transformed into another substance. Much as the impurities are burned off in a furnace, all the metaphoric funnels, strainers, and sieves were forcing me to leave behind anything inauthentic. It was at this most excruciating and intense of initiations, my soul wanted nothing less than a brand-new version of this human.

Looking back, it's now obvious that this induction paved the way for what was to become my life's sacred work. When I finally stumbled out of the spiritual crucible, I'd accomplished something rare and hard-won: a new awareness had emerged, along with a deep desire to share what I had learned to make the journey easier for others.

My tribulations had granted me a measure of wisdom, perspective, and understanding that might make other people's time in the crucible shorter, less painful, and perhaps without all the gnashing of teeth and cursing at God. If I could save someone from anguish, confusion, or fear by assisting them through the tumultuous waters I'd already navigated, it felt *essential* to do so.

I was called to support others in their awakening.

In retrospect, I am grateful for, and see how it had taken a cosmic two-by-four to the forehead to get my attention. The evolution from Air Force officer to shamanic spiritual minister, healer, teacher, and author is one helluva one-eighty! But I'm so grateful for the rewards in the form of knowing myself, locating and staying in my center, and gracefully managing my sensitive nature. Now my intuition helps me claim my power and inner authority.

That's worth every scar and every scream.

Try All Doors
by Paulette Scales

We must remember not to limit ourselves.

I'd spent my entire savings—but now I owned a beautifully remodeled mobile home in a senior's park, a place where I could truly enjoy my retirement. In this comfortable and peaceful setting, I planned to live with my little dog Paris until our last days.

My world was shattered four years later.

Without warning or legal notices, disaster struck. The mobile home park was closing! Suddenly, all of us had to make a decision: We could move our homes to a different site or abandon them.

The nightmare unraveled as the rug was pulled from beneath us. Places to move were scarce and we didn't know where to go, or exactly when the park was going to close. The park owners used scare tactics to get us to move out *now!*

Many people left, shell-shocked, and scrambled to find other accommodations. My situation was a little more complicated, as I still owed a small mortgage on my home. I had to make sure to time my move correctly.

During this difficult transition, a dear lady passed along a message from God to me. "*Ask God to open doors,*" she said. "*Investigate which doors need to be tried, to see if they might open. Don't limit yourself, even when an option appears to be out of reach.*"

God warned me, through this woman, not to be distracted by "not-for-me" thinking. I was told to have the courage to try new options, because I wouldn't need to compromise on the most important things.

My search began for a new place to call home.

Paris, my little dog, was especially intuitive and helpful at letting me know which places were not suitable. Through an internet advertisement, we found a basement suite in a nearby community that might work. The rent was a bit high, but now I knew to try "all the doors."

Though my message from God encouraged me, house hunting was a challenge. My energy was quickly depleted, making it more difficult to function. A girlfriend was kind enough to arrange appointments and handle communications for me to view the potential new homes. The three of us went together to meet the owners of the basement suite.

They were good-natured people who loved my little dog, and Paris also approved of them. The suite was beautiful and comfortable—a wonderful new home for us. Somehow, I would make the finances work. But there was one problem: The timing wasn't right.

The owners offered to hold the suite for me for one week, because they believed Paris and I were the right ones to live there. Now I had to talk to the mobile home park management about leaving the park. They put up much resistance.

My bank also was not easy to deal with concerning my situation because they insisted the mortgage be paid in full before they would release the mobile. Until I came up with the money, my former home could not be moved or even demolished.

I was caught between the park owners and the bank, and neither would budge!

My spirit was broken.

The bank seemed to be putting up more roadblocks, which made my situation even bleaker. Life looked mighty dark at that time. What does one do?

Regretfully, I had to tell the owners of the suite not to hold it for me any longer. They said again how important it was to them to get the right tenant, but even though they thought I was the one, they'd have to start showing the suite to others. They'd let me know if they found someone.

One evening, they did just that. Suitable tenants had been found and were going to sign the lease to the suite that evening. I understood and accepted this. They'd been fair to me. But I must say, because I still didn't know where I was going to live, the news was extremely discouraging.

Meanwhile, the mobile park became like a war zone.

Excavators arrived to demolish nearby mobile homes. The rumble of their heavy equipment shook the remaining homes, making some of our walls crack. The clamor was unbearable. Fewer and fewer people were left in the park now—all of us seniors—and we felt unsafe.

Another month of this went by. My friend received a call from the man who owned the basement suite, saying he happened to find her phone number and wanted to let her know that a suite across the street from him was becoming vacant. He had already mentioned my situation to his neighbors, and they were waiting to hear from us.

The three of us—my girlfriend, my dog, and me—met with the owners of the place across the street and viewed the available suite. It was perfect! Even the price was right. From that moment forward, everything began to flow.

Timing is everything!

In our lovely new suite, both my little dog Paris and I found peace. We lived in that tranquil space for almost five years. During this time, I was gifted with words to write a children's book about Paris and her best friend, which I self-published and dedicated to my grandson.

And the new home came with a bonus: Now we were only a few minutes' drive from where my friend lived. Both my little dog and I got to revel in the beauty of nature in her lush, green backyard. How special!

If I had remained in my mobile home—if they had let me stay—I'd never have discovered this new and wonderful path. I might have missed all the different kinds of physical and emotional healing that became part of my life.

Thinking back on all the desperation I felt as the mobile home park was crumbling around me, I'm filled with gratitude. Those challenges taught me to be patient and to trust the process of life.

Trying all doors can be utilized in many different areas of change in life. We must remember not to limit ourselves.

Downsizing: A Life-Changing Roller Coaster Ride

by Peggy Linsey

Cherished memories are much more valuable than stuff.

I will beat this monster, I vow. "It won't paralyze me!"

Like many other Baby Boomers, we had realized that moving to a smaller house made sense. Our decision unleashed the *downsizing monster*. The monster's awakening has released chaos as we fight through an emotional tug-of-war accompanied by countless hours of back-breaking work.

Colliding emotions lurk in every box and closet we open.

I tell myself it is only *stuff*. Downsizing is about getting rid of *stuff*—my precious *stuff*.

My research has advised that, to effectively and efficiently downsize, the first stage is decluttering. I start by combing through a stack of outdated magazines here, a pile of dusty books there, flinging several things into boxes. These safe and simple targets help ease my way into the massive chore ahead.

Decluttering the reading material is accomplished with surprising ease. My emotional roller coaster is under control at this point, entering a slow climb as I offhandedly discard items that do not have too much time or too many emotional memories engraved on them. By starting slowly, I postpone the terror of the impending twists and turns.

But eventually, the roller coaster reaches the summit. Now my job requires touching every-single-thing-I-own and making quick decisions: what to keep, throw away, sell, or donate. My mantra becomes, "If we were moving tomorrow, would we take it with us—or not?"

As I divide the contents of our house into these categories, I know our *keep* pile is growing far too bulky. My husband helps whittle it down by earmarking some of his important *things*—like his record album collection—for donation.

Even decluttering has several layers to it. Some things have to be evaluated a second or even third time.

Conflicting emotions—discouragement, overwhelm, relief, and pride—wash over me.

As the emotional roller coaster begins its descent, we encounter hairpin turns. My decluttering project moves deeper into our dark corners, closets, and storage boxes. The monster waits at every turn as we consider the contents of the basement and finally the attic. By this point, emotions overwhelm me as I ask myself, "How can I do all this?"

But the next day finds me with new-found energy, breaking up the job into manageable tasks—such as working on one shelf at a time, rather than the whole closet. I enjoy a sense of accomplishment with the completion of each tiny task. But it is not long before I realize the job will get tougher before it gets easier.

Eventually, the roller coaster does a loop-dee-loop into Walks Down Memory Lane.

New, more intense emotions percolate to the surface, often unexpectedly, as we explore mystery storage containers and closets.

What can possibly be in this box? I wonder.

It's photographs of Mom and Dad, and my father's military discharge papers. These documents are particularly somber to view. My heart aches—but scanning and sharing some of these items with my siblings makes Mom and Dad come alive again, and that gives me peace. The photos are repackaged as *keepers*.

Sometimes I laugh at what turns up, like the day I discover a lost car key in a coat pocket. "The missing car key! That's where it was all these years!" More often, though, long-forgotten, once-but-no-longer-meaningful items are discovered which results in another tear or two, or even outright sobbing.

My children's crumpled baby clothes. The handmade-by-me tiny Halloween and dance recital costumes. Their colorful sports teams' shirts. Not *all* of these can find a spot in the keep pile, so I begin photographing them, hoping pictures will help preserve the associated memories for me. Once I've gotten a grip on myself, I admit that these items can still bring happiness to other children, and they are gently and lovingly placed in our give-away pile.

As I continue strolling down *Memory Lane, and the Roller Coaster Ride,* I'll need broader shoulders and tougher skin. One minute, I'm impressed with myself for finding the fortitude to discard a treasured item, like my box of playbills from every theatrical performance I've ever attended. But, later that night, awakened by regret, I sneak out to retrieve the playbills from the trash.

Eventually, I do release them. Some things just take longer.

Another day, another bout of emotional turmoil. Happiness, grief, relief, and melancholy storm through as I discover yet more memories from stuff that must be relinquished.

We sell much of our furniture, pocketing the proceeds to buy different things for the new house. This eases the brief clutch of pain as I let go of our dining room set, the gathering place where our growing family celebrated holidays and commemorated births and deaths.

However, the day the new owners of our piano roll it out of our house, the lump that spontaneously forms in my throat triggers an episode of crying. Who could have predicted this sudden, overwhelming sadness? Somehow, losing this piano reveals the stark reality of our decision to move to a smaller home, where a piano will not fit.

The memories of hearing our children practice their lessons and prepare for their recitals creep up, and they floor me. Yes, another family will enjoy creating similar memories. I find some solace in that—but these musical memories will pull on my heartstrings for as long as I live.

Eventually, some areas are cleared out. Genuine feelings of relief start to manifest.

Each finished box or bin triggers a sense of cleansing. Now, every clear shelf or closet energizes me to keep going—despite the emotional roller coaster's rapid drops and climbs that flip us upside down. The monster is relentless!

We rent a huge trash receptacle, which will squat in our yard for two weeks. Our goal is to fill it to the very top. Its contents will be going to the "burial ground" at the dump, so we give careful consideration to any item we toss inside, given their fate.

An old workbench that belonged to my deceased father-in-law occupies one corner of our basement. It even has a vintage vice grip bolted to the surface. Dumping it as trash would break my heart, again, so I decide to list it for sale. Numerous buyers show interest in this relic! We make money with its sale, and I am thrilled to know it will have a new useful, life for its new owners.

We start making weekly trips to the local thrift store with donations. It is cathartic to realize that other people might love our outgrown clothes, slightly used furniture, and well-loved toys. We might no longer need them, but they still have a purpose. This realization is comforting.

As the claws of the downsizing monster dig deeper, the roller coaster ride takes more insane turns, plunging us into melancholy and then soaring to high motivation. I must continue purging. But heart-wrenching tasks lay ahead. We realize we'll need to let go of some of our children's favorite toys: the colorful play kitchen, the well-used basketball hoop, and a box of imaginative dress-up clothes. We snap photos of school projects and faded posters to ease the misery of discarding these innocent days-gone-by. Some dolls and a dollhouse, certain souvenir baseballs, and a few board games are tagged as *keepers* … for now.

Our home starts to look more vacant. Memories echo like our voices in its sparse rooms. I try to envision the house as more spacious, not emptier. Emotionally and physically exhausted, we sink down onto the bare floor and laugh until we cry.

We invite the monster to join us, but it feels beaten and declines.

"I must keep my sense of humor," I tell myself, but my senses detect that these rooms now look, sound, and smell foreign without their décor. The closets seem so different with empty hangers rattling around on the poles.

When we carry the packed "keeper" boxes and our remaining furniture out of the house, the monster emerges one last time—but it seems confused and less menacing now. I am challenged to soul-search, and motivated to make it to the finish line.

And then, this enormous project— decluttering, packing, and moving—is over, for one single reason: Our time runs out.

Somewhere along the way, we were successful. We downsized.

These days, my feelings of liberation from *stuff* far outweigh any sadness or discouragement I encountered on my wild and crazy ride. It's a relief to know our children will not have their own emotional roller coaster of cleaning out their parents' lifelong home. We can retire now, knowing we have completed a significant life-job.

The raging monster has been vanquished. The ride's metal wheels have slowed down to a softly rumbling crawl.

We are free to spend our time now doing things we choose to do, without the enormous burden of so much *stuff* cluttering our minds and weighing on our shoulders or our hearts. I can proudly announce to our Baby Boomer friends, "I did it. I downsized—and lived to write about it."

A Divine Mother and a Pearl
by Altair Shyam

"God bless you. I love you."

The sound of shouting, a clamor steadily rising into a battle cry, came from the far end of the courtyard. I heard the ringing of bells—a terrible sound, not like the sound of a bell calling people to church, but the clanging of many bells crying out in fear as they were bludgeoned to death. The courtyard had become a scene of devastation.

The courtyard walls now opened, revealing a horizon torn ragged by dense, mottled brown mountains. The Light grew more intense. The hidden veils trembled and parted above me and to left and right, like curtains drawn back against time. The arcs swirled around me, increasing in brilliance and magnificence, right across the horizon until they touched the lips of the sky itself. I could hear the hiss and fiery bellows of vast, unimaginable forces forging weapons for battle.

"Soldiers!" came a cry.

The cry was not in my own tongue, but in a language and voice that was both strange yet familiar. I knew, with a mixture of joy and trepidation, that my own mouth had spoken the word. A sudden force propelled me forward, knocking the breath from me, and I could only pant and gasp as bullets rang overhead, ricocheting off prayer bells. The thick, whitewashed mud-brick walls of the monastery were no defense.

I stood above the eggshell-colored sands of the courtyard, in front of the monastery's main temple. Impossible! I thought as another round of artillery clattered off the heavily damaged doors of the temple's central gate.

Strained voices barked severe orders. The monks, clearly trained for fighting, moved into a defensive formation, but they were hopelessly outnumbered and outgunned by the soldiers pouring through onto the temple grounds from the streets beyond. The soldiers were heavily armed. The monks, who wielded farming implements and short kitchen knives, could only fight at close range. And so, they waited, vulnerable to snipers and attacks from the air. Though the monks exploded with fury when the soldiers came closer, so many fell—wasted lives and helpless victims in a rebellion not of their choosing.

I was dragged back inside the temple gates and now stood above the thick, wooden doors with their beautiful brass ornaments. An arcade swept along the interior wall, which was alive with many ancient pictures of Buddhas, painted in extraordinary detail with flower petals that gently melded together, portraying Buddha's robes folding so precisely and intricately. I watched in horror as the first wave of Chinese soldiers defaced the frescoes as they ran past, gouging and hacking the face of every Buddha from the plaster.

I looked up at a burst of fire in the sky. Artillery shells smashed into the columned prayer and chanting hall. The hall faced a huge altar of sacred symbols flanked by eight towering, gold-painted images of the Buddha.

Tiny yellow flames in front of each statue flickered and then died out as if signaling the death knell of the heart of the temple. The innumerable brass bowls brimming with cloudy yak butter were pitched and tossed into the carnage. Their thick, sweet fragrance—mixed with the odor of blood and the toxic fumes of spent artillery shells—hung heavy in the dim light.

If I'd thought I had time to get my bearings, I was mistaken. Another shell blasted through the wall on the opposite side of the courtyard and opened to a vista of squat stone buildings. Leafless trees sporadically skewering the landscape burst into flames as the soldiers passed.

Peering in the direction the shell had come from, I saw platoons of soldiers on their way to join the ones already looting the temple, and in the radiance of the Light, I was dragged out of the fray by this same invisible force.

I saw myself as a monk standing on a bridge as a companion and I looked out over a vast chasm.

A terrifying scream struck my heart with dread.

My scream. Soldiers standing in formation to block any exit from the bridge had opened fire. As I watched, a bright line marked the track of the bullet that pierced my heart.

I pitched off the side of the bridge and fell headlong into the chasm below. The soldiers were following so quickly that they swept past where my companion lay, crumpled, ghost-like. Their target was the temple at the center of the monastery, and they ran straight toward it without hesitating or turning to the side. More artillery shells flew overhead, ripping straight through the remaining walls and devastating the buildings within.

None of this mattered to me. The Light was becoming transparent and the veil between my own time and that horrid memory was fading. My heart lay like a stone within my body. Distant figures still ran through the monastery; their bodies tottered and fell as they were cut down in flames. What had been a temple was now a mass of twisted wood and metal, a pall of smoke rising from its center.

The bridge, bearing the weight of so much carnage, creaked and cracked open, and then collapsed into the chasm after me.

I fell, screaming, as the mighty sound of OM resounded around me and the Light grew closer. I screamed again. With a loud crash, the last remnants of that horrid scene below fell into the abyss.

I was floating, perfectly still. Looking down, I could see my body lying prone on the bed, bathed in the early morning sunshine. The veil was still there. I didn't want to return, but with enormous effort, pushed until I was gliding just above my body. One breath, then another, and my Light Body rolled back into the side of the body on the bed. I landed back in the physical realm with a soft thump and heard a whoosh, as if all the air was being pressed from my lungs. My body heaved as I took a deep breath.

After a moment, my eyes opened. I dug my nails into my sweat-soaked bed sheets, to make sure I was home.

I'd been having the same dream every night for the last year. Now my mother was beside me, soothing me as she did every morning. Those vivid dreams returned, night after night.

She would tuck me into bed and sing to me, and together we would pray to Jesus with the Archangels Auriel, Gabriel, Raphael, and Michael.

Four Angels round my head.
Four angels at my bed.
One to watch and one to pray,
And two to guide my soul this day.

My mother's protection and love of Jesus helped me endure the hard times.

This dream and my mother's love helped me begin to make a big inner change when I was still a child. My heart was able to connect the seed of light and love—that same light of the universe, from my dream—with the pure love of the Mother that each of us carries within. Although I was bullied at school, right through to my teenage years, my inner world of light and love was stronger than any external circumstances.

My mother had told me from birth that, in addition to Jesus—whom I absolutely adored—I was protected by the Virgin Mary. She said the Divine Mother would appear to me in many forms over my lifetime. She was right. I have been blessed and graced by the constant protection and divine embrace of the Mother.

Sai Baba has a gift for you.

Many years later, while walking in a local shopping area with my girlfriend Aria, a woman walking past stopped and gave us her card.

"My name is Shanti," she said. "Sai Baba wants you to come and visit him at my sacred shrine. He has a gift for you. He has been waiting for you."

So that afternoon, Aria and I found the house, which was just above the beach, and knocked on the door. The same woman who had met us earlier bowed and welcomed us in.

"Follow me," she said.

We climbed down the basement steps behind her. Two statues sat in pools of what appeared to be water. The first statue depicted Ganesha, the god of good fortune, remover of obstacles, and patron of the arts, sciences, and wisdom. Out of his trunk poured a golden nectar for which I could see no obvious source. Shanti pointed to the large bowl now overflowing with the liquid, which dripped onto plastic sheets on the floor.

"Taste it," she said. "Nectar from Heaven. Amrita. The Ambrosia of Immortality. To taste it is to attain higher knowledge and power."

I did taste it. It was sweet, not like honey or sugar, but a different sweetness altogether, with the lightness and glow of heaven. Then I turned to the second statue, which was of Guan Yin.

"Kneel down and pray to her," said Shanti. "If Divine Mother Guan Yin is willing and you touch her heart with compassion, she will give you a priceless gift."

I knelt and prayed, knowing I'd been waiting a long time for this moment.

"Hold out your hands," said Shanti.

As I stretched out my cupped hands under the Heart of Guan Yin's statue, an amazing miracle occurred. The most beautiful pearl began to grow From the Heart of Guan Yin. It emerged little by little, like a baby from the womb of her heart. To my astonishment, I saw the lustrous pearl was attached to the statue's heart by a thin strand of pearly silk, like a baby's umbilical cord connected to its mother's body. Gradually, the weight of the pearl allowed the silk strand to stretch and lower the pearl. Then the strand broke, depositing the pearl in my hands.

"You must have been a monk," said Shanti. "When I traveled to see Sai Baba, he guided me to a monastery in Sri Lanka where his monks had prayed over this statue for years. They gave me the statue and told me to use it to heal the world. They said it had great powers of manifestation and miracles and would recognize a person by the power of his compassionate heart. To some, Guan Yin would give a chintamani stone—a wish-fulfilling jewel."

My eyes filled with tears of gratitude. I bowed deeply to the Divine Mother in all Her forms, just as my own mother had, and offered deep and reverent thanks for this miracle.

Many years after the Divine Mother gave the pearl to me, I knew it was time to let it go.

I had used the stone for many years for healing. One day, my wife told me it was time to let it go. "It has served its purpose," she said. "The healing of Divine Mother is in you now."

I knew she was right. My Mum at that stage had been quite ill, so I brought the stone to her and left it in her care. I knew it would not be long until her time for transition was complete.

Change. The biggest transformation we make is when we pass from this life to the next.

When Mum passed, I was on the "night watch." We were alone, in the serenity and space of peace, as she took her last breath. Her transition was a beautiful and moving experience for me.

I had awakened suddenly at 4:06 a.m. to find her breathing had become shallow. So, I knew it was time. I reminded her that she had given birth to me around this time, and that she was now going to rebirth herself with the angels' help, in God's Light. I watched her holding Dad's hand all the way back to heaven. Then her breathing stopped.

As I clasped her hand, I told her, "God bless you. I love you."

Then she was gone, onto her next great journey. She didn't take the pearl with her, but to this day, I have no idea where it disappeared to.

It was such a privilege and an honor to be with my mother, to hold her hand and let her know everything was okay. As she had helped me, I was able to help her let go, surrender, and return home.

The Power of True Self-Expression
by Cassandra A. Tindal

Your voice is one of the most important things you will ever own. You have the ability to make waves, and to shake up the world we live in.

As a young girl, my parents raised me to be seen (or not) and seldom heard. Because I was just a kid, I followed the rules: sit quietly, keep my mouth shut, and mind my own business unless someone asks a question.

Now I believe my parents were passing along the rules of their own painful pasts and recreating their enforced silence. They had learned the best way to cope with their feelings was by keeping a tight lip. The cycle repeated. They expected me to keep a certain part of myself unheard and invisible.

My childhood rules eventually crystalized into attitudes and behavioral patterns that engrained themselves into my psyche and guided my life. I went from needing to withdraw as a child to being withdrawn as a teen, and then as an adult. My inability to express my views had a serious effect on my life. I was never certain what to question, because I felt defenseless.

Childhood memories stick with me for life.

Being powerless was a lonesome feeling. Because my family considered crying a sign of weakness, I learned to bottle up feelings of pain or anger. I always had to appear strong and in control of my emotions.

When my father died, whom I loved dearly, I began to sob. My brother, now considered the man of the house, told me to stop crying and rudely said, "Shut up!"

I wanted to scream with grief from the deep sorrow I felt, but wasn't allowed to, at least not openly. I'll never forget how at that moment in time I learned to suppress the experience of a very painful emotion. From that day forward I wondered if I needed permission to express natural human emotions.

My early training left me feeling inadequate and unimportant. I didn't get to experience enough verbal, social interactions because I was never acknowledged when I tried to communicate emotions.

I grew up accustomed to people ignoring my value and overlooking what I had to "bring to the table." That made it especially daunting for me to gather my confidence and speak what was on my mind. I still struggle sometimes with worrying about how others perceive me. Questioning my worth has made me back away from a few challenges and opportunities. At times, I wonder, *Am I good enough?*

Finally, I found a little bit of hope.

It happened during junior high school. My classmates and I were asked to write our thoughts about what the word "hope" meant to us. This was my chance. I was being given permission to express what had been repressed for so long. I wrote these simple words: *Hope is the breath of a dying man!*

To my surprise, out of all the submissions, mine—yes, mine! —was selected for inclusion in my graduating class yearbook. I had won. My voice had been heard. I'd expressed myself in a beautiful and positive way for all to hear.

This small success inspired me. Finally, *I had hope*. My thoughts mattered, and I felt freer to express myself. For the first time in my life, I felt empowered. That's when I began unraveling those insecure feelings and thoughts and began trying to believe in my self-worth.

I was already valuable. I just needed to recognize my value. This is the process of building self-worth.

Fearing my voice had crippled me. Hearing my voice freed me from the fear of speaking out and sharing my emotions. It was a healing experience. The more I listened to my voice and shared my opinions, the more my character became defined. I began to deeply understand myself, what made me tick, and what I could contribute.

With these wonderful pieces of knowledge, I became a real individual.

Following my breast cancer diagnosis, I had to make the most courageous decision of my life. This was a scary time for me. The doctors told me my cancer was aggressive and gave me a severe treatment plan. They dictated what was going to happen, and that was it—no discussion.

Fear overwhelmed me. What would happen to my child if I died? Thinking there were no other options, I went along with the treatment plan: to cut and poison the cancer. But after my second chemotherapy treatment, my gut instinct told me to stop.

It took courage to trust my own intuition. But the voice speaking to me from inside my soul sent a clear message that could not be ignored.

Forces much greater than us are always present to empower and guide us in making the right choices for our lives. I had to trust in that power—

the power of my creator, the One who had created this body in the first place.

Although I was convinced my inner voice was right, I still needed to muster the courage to tell my doctors I was canceling the remaining treatment plan, because of my instincts. Sometimes, when we listen to our own voice, it tells us to take a leap of faith toward what we know to be true. My medical team opposed my decision, but I never wavered.

Without any further treatment, eleven years later, I am here to tell my story.

This experience taught me to trust in my spiritual voice, to be courageous, and to have confidence in what I truly believe. Ignoring my voice and silencing my beliefs or emotions had been an early message, but it was bad advice. Feeling leads to healing. When I pushed away, suppressed, or criticized myself for having emotions, the cost was too high: my health.

It's a great time to be a woman.

As a woman, I realize how important it is to break through the bondage of my own fears and give myself the opportunity to be heard. That's how I can create social change. The power of women's self-expression, opinions, and ideas has never been acknowledged more openly than it is today. Our power can have a profound impact. It is true, times are changing for women.

But why has it taken so long? The problem began many years ago. Society's long-held beliefs, cultures, and traditions have muted women.

Speaking up has required women to develop courage and confidence. Taking control by voice rather than by force can be scary. But as we build enough confidence to do what is necessary, we grow stronger.

If you have ever been told that your voice and your views don't matter—that was a lie! Your voice is one of your most valuable possessions, and with it, you can shake up our world.

Instead of making excuses, use your gifts to make a change.

Growing Wings:
The Complex Path to a Simple Life
by Sora Garrett

Change is messy, and it transforms us in ways
that we never expect and can never plan.

I'm sitting in the middle of my new life, and it looks nothing like I had imagined.

The house is aged and outdated, with boring white walls, garish brass doorknobs, and ugly wallpaper borders. It might have looked beautiful to the elderly previous 80's-something owners, but not to me. And there's a musty smell coming from the carpet.

Sigh. What had promised to be an exhilarating opportunity to transform someone else's living space into our own now feels like an overwhelming chore.

In an attempt to adjust my mood, I turn my gaze outside to the expansive yard. This was the real reason we chose this property when it became clear we needed to move. Now all I see out there is work: a vast lawn where I'll need to plant more trees, a tangle of overgrown grapevines, and straggly, over-pruned bushes. A neglected, uneven rock path cuts straight through the yard—leading to nothing.

Viewing the property has made me feel even more discouraged.

My heart is heavy with grief as my mind spins, casting about with uncertainty. What started out as a smart choice to right-size our life is starting to feel like a devastating mistake.

Why did we decide to make this move? I know the answer, but today I'm full of resentment about the circumstances that brought us here.

I had loved our splendid home in town, the space we built with such creativity and joy. It sat in my favorite part of town, close to friends, nature walks, and my new grandson. I think of him and start to cry.

I miss my grandson, even though he's not that far away. Spending time with him is more complicated now. I can't simply stroll over and escort him to our favorite park when his dad needs a helping hand. Now we have to coordinate schedules, add an hour for the drive, and find someplace to hang out that isn't a remodeling mess.

I remind myself that this change was a choice.

It was a choice that came after we began to feel the effects of a weakened economy that had significantly changed our financial foundation. Not only was our retirement plan compromised, but we were both self-employed, so the ripples of impact began to weaken the foundations of our life, causing us to worry and stress over money in a way we had never done before.

It wasn't easy, but we decided to sell our cherished home and move to a smaller one in a rural community outside of town. We weren't going too far, so it was easy to pretend that not much would change. Our family and friends, our favorite diners and walking routes would still be relatively close. And of course, we would still have each other. I try to persuade my heart to stop aching.

216

Why does it hurt so much to change?

Moving is even more complicated when one of you is going through menopause. Maybe that's why this change has been so devastating. Some days, I barely know myself within this silently real transformation, its emotional roller coaster taking me through deeper cycles of depression and irritability than I have ever known. Today is one of those days. I let more tears fall.

My husband is also going through a couple of health challenges that are causing extra worry and stress. His energy is lower than usual, which is making this remodel take longer than either of us had expected. It's hard to be angry with him when I know he's not feeling well. But some days, like today, I am angry.

Does some part of me blame him for this change? It was more my fault than his. He tried to liquidate our stock portfolio before the stock market fell, and I didn't want to buy into the fear, so I resisted. How I wish I could change *that* decision!

I take a deep breath and try to grant myself forgiveness.

One of the reasons we decided to move was that it would give us more financial freedom. Maybe this change is trying to teach me that real security can't be found in material things. *Didn't I already learn that lesson?*

Closing my eyes, I connect with the deeper part of me that understands the point of every lesson. My heart relaxes open, and I can feel more space inside my head. The light returns.

My thoughts drift to my aging in-laws, who are going through an even more devastating change. My mother-in-love is beginning to lose her mind. Her husband has a hard time coping with the idea that, on some days, she doesn't seem to recognize him. Her sons and daughter are beginning to lose the mom they have always known.

Her changing brain adds a different kind of stress in our lives. Arrangements can be interrupted with a single phone call, so every plan is tentative. With jumbled emotions, we consider memory care. Our hearts break as we helplessly watch Alzheimer's change her personality. I hate to admit this, even to myself, but some days I wish she would simply let go and save us from the painful passage of watching her fade away.

I try to fetch that thought back, but it's there, so what am I to do? Recalling her smile and her incredibly generous heart, I offer up my gratitude for her life.

When I close my eyes, I can't shake the feeling that something inside me is dying. Perhaps it's true. The caterpillar has to spin its cocoon and plunge into total darkness before it can transform. I've heard that the insect's new "imaginal cells" have to devour the old cells as part of this transformation. Today, it certainly feels like I'm being devoured as I unwillingly submit to the changes around me.

Ultimately, change always offers a choice.

This is what I must remind myself: It might not be apparent, but choice is always here. We can learn and move into the new or remain stuck in the old. We can choose to embrace the change, or resist it—but eventually, things will change anyway.

As a highly creative person, change can beckon me, opening new possibilities and refreshing what has been. I sometimes say I'm a serial entrepreneur because each business venture helps me grow. And since creative people don't like to remain still for too long, we *create* change!

But this time, my feelings of resistance and resentment have been staggering, rocking me to my core. After all, I had *chosen* to make this not-really-that-big change. *Where did all those emotional layers come from?*

Like the caterpillar, I had to go into my cocoon to let the new devour the old, and it truly has transformed me. As I made time to *be* with the change, to invite it to change the way I was holding onto the past, the messiness returned to order, beauty, and spaciousness.

But this transformation was harder than I could have imagined. What I realize now is that I was accepting the change on the surface only. Underneath, there was resistance, resentment, and regret. Because even though it began with a *choice* to change, I was still hanging on. I kept feeling I had lost something, and the more I felt that loss, the more I resisted the change. Until I could fully *embrace* the change, it had control over me. I can see that now.

But what do I do with the changes I don't actually want? Maybe I don't have to embrace all those changes, but I *do* need to accept the change and keep growing *with* the change, which may mean choosing to do something to create a *different* change. <grin>

When I allow myself to be changed by life, in all its richness and complexity, and accept even the struggle — maybe *especially* the struggle — I am transformed.

The caterpillar may not be aware of her next emergence as a beautiful butterfly, but she still spins herself into a dark cocoon. I may not have chosen to go through all these changes at the same time, but that's the way they came.

Life is change, and every change brings new life. It takes a simple choice to move with the change, rather than against it; even when that means embracing the struggle. This is how we grow wings.

I open my eyes to see a butterfly fluttering among the flowers just outside the window. This time, when I look at my new, enormous backyard, I smile. The sunroom's floor-to-ceiling windows bathe me in the day's light. I detect a spark of inspiration about this house's possibilities.

Maybe the complexity of all these changes is God's way of strengthening me for opportunities I haven't yet imagined. A flutter in my heart makes me realize this is probably true.

I can almost feel a new pair of strong, transparent wings beginning to emerge.

In Search of More with Less

by Dennis Pitocco

Life begins at the end of your comfort zone.

There I sat, thinking: *What now? What's next? Where do we go from here? Would I disappoint her?* More on that later.

Everyone seemed to focus on writing about, talking about, and dreaming about achieving that elusive "work/life balance." Although their reasoning seemed to consistently recommend the benefits of achieving this balance, we knew it rarely happened, and even more rarely did such balance last.

No matter how well-intentioned they were, everyone appeared to fail.

But not us! After years of "kicking the can down the road," the time had finally come. We were going to disconnect from our everyday life so we could reconnect with each other and the world around us.

We were going to do it not just for us, but for friends and family who might be inspired to follow our walk-the-talk lead someday.

So began our search to discover a way to do "more with less."

My wife and I didn't know that our quest would ultimately result in an actual walk down the infamous Camino de Santiago (known in English as the Way of Saint James.) The Camino de Santiago is a pilgrimage route that leads to Santiago de Compostela, where the remains of Saint James (Santiago) were discovered in the ninth century.

The route has become popular in recent years. Many people find the exertion of walking for weeks—and being disconnected from modern devices for all that time—immensely liberating. Some see it as a spiritual path or a retreat for their spiritual growth.

We decided to walk the last 205 miles of the Camino de Santiago— starting in Leon, Spain and traveling to the city of Santiago de Compostela— in our search for something more.

An allegory for life itself, the Camino is a long and winding road that one must travel one step at a time.

The genesis for this adventure had been dinner with a long-lost friend in Phoenix who told us about the movie *The Way,* which inspired him to plan a trip to Spain to scatter the ashes of his recently deceased son. By carrying the ashes along the infamous Camino de Santiago and spilling them into the North Atlantic Ocean, he would honor his son and give emotional closure to his grief.

Call it karma. Call it coincidence. The next evening, my wife and I watched the movie and were inspired to add the trip to our own "disconnect bucket list." Four years later, our inspiration became a reality.

On an overcast and windy day, our pilgrimage started in the village of Valverde de la Virgen, just outside of Leon. As we took our first steps on the trail, we experienced a little of the storied camaraderie that exists among travelers. The friendly locals wished us *"Buen camino,"* the traditional greeting for pilgrims that translates to "good path" or "good road."

Our beginning walking pace was brisk as we followed the yellow arrows that guide pilgrims along the route. It surprised us how quickly we became accustomed to spotting these arrows, wherever they turned up. Some are up high on posts and some are on the street. They're painted on walls, and some even appear bending around corners!

The walk kept us engaged. Sometimes we passed by others, and sometimes they passed us. Everyone we met was friendly, and we often heard the customary *"Buen camino."*

We quickly realized how important it is to walk at your own pace and make the trip your own.

Although we had prepared for our journey with a small supply of food and water, each little town along the way had a cafe or restaurant offering snacks and drinks. We decided to stop halfway through the day at Villandangos del Paramo, where we could take the advice of many who have gone before us: to rest, eat, and remove our boots for a while.

As my boots came off, I was quite surprised to discover a few small blisters on my feet, although I'd felt no real discomfort during our morning walk. We both were proud of how well we had planned this aspect of the trip. Not only did we purchase the ideal walking boots, as recommended by the experts, but we had slowly and steadily broken those boots in over the course of many walks during the year as we trained for our journey. Nevertheless, we also carried a package of adhesive bandages, just in case. Now we simply covered each blister carefully, to ensure comfort for the remainder of the day's trek.

After the brief respite, off we went again, covering another eight miles of majestic beauty and boundless serenity. As we trekked up and down the hills and valleys, we were astonished by breathtaking views of nature at its very best, a world uncompromised by man or machine.

As our trek continued, I was surprised to feel burning sensations on the bottoms of both my feet, as if they were being pinched with each step I took. But we soldiered on, unwilling to be deterred by a blister or two.

Our final stop for the day was Hospital de Orbigo. According to legend, in 1434, a knight challenged other knights to cross the bridge there and break three lances against him, all to impress a lady. Thankfully, we were not required to deal with any lances. We arrived at our lodging around 3:30 p.m., delighted to have an opportunity to rest for the evening. We anticipated a much longer journey—twenty-seven plus miles—the next day.

We were relieved to remove our now-christened walking boots and relax while we enjoyed a pilgrim's three-course dinner, accompanied by local wine. Before settling down for the night, we attended to my feet by popping whatever blisters we could and soaking my feet in the bathtub for as long as possible.

We spent a challenging night in an unfamiliar bed. Both of my feet burned without ceasing. But by morning, the pain had given way to a gorgeous sunrise, and we knew a world of discovery lay ahead. We dressed my feet as best we could, and off we went again.

I walked gingerly now and with the help of a collapsible walking stick I'd originally intended to use climbing hills along the trail. Throughout the day, we discovered not only amazing scenery, steeped in history and legend, but also the simple pleasures of life stripped back to the essentials.

As the hours went by, we strolled through several small villages, ultimately taking a break about four miles into our journey, driven not by a need for rest or snacks but because I felt that my feet were on fire. I came upon a stone bench on the outskirts of the village and took the opportunity to pull off my boots and explore the condition of my feet.

There I sat. Boots off. Feet exposed. *What now? What's next?*

Where do we go from here? Would I disappoint her? These tough questions arose swiftly when I discovered that the previous day's blisters had now morphed into scarlet bubbles covering the soles of both feet—festering, multiplying blisters. It became glaringly obvious I simply couldn't put my boots back on. In fact, it looked like I was on the precipice of ending my trip, just ten miles into our long-planned, 205-mile adventure.

As my wife approached on the road from the village, she saw me look up from inspecting my feet. She said later that she'd never witnessed such an overwhelming look of anguish and despair. We both realized that tough choices lay ahead.

The most obvious and likely best choice would be to terminate our journey right there and then. We knew we could hire a taxi from the village to drive us back to where this junket began.

Even getting my socks back on would be a test of my pain threshold. My feet were well beyond band-aid solutions. We knew that I couldn't keep walking in my "ideal" boots but finding alternative footwear in the village seemed nearly impossible because of my exceptionally large shoe size.

Not one to give up hope, my wife decided to venture back into the local hamlet in search of anything resembling a shoe store. Although I appreciated her noble effort, any steps forward, regardless of what covered my feet, were going to be torment and potentially dangerous to my health.

So, there I sat, pondering the smartest and most logical choice—retreat—and weighing it against the years of anticipation, planning, and excitement that had gone into this bucket-list adventure.

I couldn't let her down. I couldn't let us down. There had to be a way.

What I needed at this point was a purpose to go on. At the end of the Camino de Santiago, many pilgrims are asked, "What was the reason for your walk?" The answers people give are as individual as they are varied. Some do it for spiritual renewal, and others to escape their daily life and reconnect with nature. Some are looking for a challenge, or for exercise, or to explore a different culture.

Our original reason had been a combination of all of the above, I suppose, ultimately centered on three words: escape, unplug, and renew. But now I would need to dig deeper, to find some personal goal to propel me forward over the remaining 195 miles.

This was the time to fall upon my faith and beg for Divine intervention. And that's when thoughts of my sister Dee came into my consciousness.

My beloved sister, one of seven siblings, had passed away too young, just nine years earlier, following a long illness. She was an amazing woman who embraced her faith and loved her family until the end.

I decided, then and there, that my reason for conquering my pain and completing the pilgrimage would be to honor my sister. I would "do it for Dee."

The instant I made this decision, my wife came strolling back from the village with news: She had discovered just one small shoe shop, about a half mile down the road. I would have to join her, so the proprietor could do his best to find something that would fit my inflamed feet.

Without new footwear, my journey for Dee would be over before it started. I hobbled into the village, now with help from both of our walking sticks, sharing my newfound inspiration with my wife along the way.

The shopkeeper, who spoke no English, understood at a glance that there was no point in measuring my feet. He just needed to locate the largest shoes in his shop. Hoping for the best, he rummaged through his inventory.

There were no size-thirteen shoes to be found; his largest were size ten. But then he remembered the only pair of sandals in his shop, which perched in the window display. He slid the sandals onto my feet in one last effort to solve our problem.

And it worked! They fit, but only because of the long, adjustable Velcro straps. These sandals would be able to expand to whatever width I needed to snugly hold my feet in place, without putting any pressure on my damaged skin.

Fairytales do come true. Miracles *do* happen.

Energized by what we genuinely believed to be Divine intervention, our walk continued, mile by mile. I had to frequently stop to adjust my Velcro straps, and the pain was ever-present, but so was my desire to keep moving forward—no matter what.

Night after night, we checked into a villa and I made my way to the bathtub to soak my feet. Morning after morning, my wife inspected each foot and then dressed my wounds carefully with whatever ointment she had found that day.

While the blisters ultimately claimed every inch of my feet, we soldiered on. My pace would be close to a crawl for the first thirty minutes of each day, but then I would find a steady rhythm. We avoided any notion of stopping once forward motion was in gear, fearing that the agonizing, feet-on-fire sensation might provide too great a temptation to stop for good.

Twelve days, 205 miles, and 485,866 painful steps later, we reached the Santiago de Compostela. A monk staffing the arrival counter did indeed ask, "What was the reason for your walk?"

My reply? "I did it for Dee."

Over the years since then, many people have inquired about our experience. What did we learn? Did the walk change our lives? Would we do it again? Our answers are always the same.

We were grateful to have learned so much more about each other. Not only had we faced down a crisis, but we'd spent hours upon hours together each day, experiencing glorious nature coupled with quiet serenity. We rid ourselves of every post-it note that had been stored in our brains over the years, every story we had never shared, and every unspoken word. We'd embraced hours of disconnected silence. We had learned that life begins at the end of your comfort zone.

In the end, we were changed by having this opportunity to think about each other, about our friends, and about our families.

We returned home with a newfound understanding of what really mattered, which helped us decide where we were going to invest our precious time from that point forward. And as the title to this story portends, together, we found a way to have more with less.

Would we ever do it again? It took slightly more than six months for the skin on my feet to heal completely. Over time, our thoughts of returning to the Camino de Santiago began to surface. Yes, we are going back there next year. We will undertake the same journey—but with different shoes.

We'll also have a different perspective. We have been enriched by the wisdom of our last experience and blessed by the opportunity to do it one more time, "for Dee."

Final Thoughts

The long and winding road to clarity in life begins with the first step, no matter how big or small. We are never alone on our journey because we are the hero who can always stand with us, on our travel toward peace of mind because no matter where we go, there we are.

Former CBS anchorman Walter Cronkite[1] sought solitude to reconnect with his inner self for clarity. Author James Michener reported he found peace by walking his dogs on deserted paths. According to the recent Mayo Clinic Research[2], positive thinking helps with stress management and can even improve our health.

When the psyche is at peace, the body often follows. Our worst state of chaos might just be a gift in disguise. Upheaval may offer the opportunity to make life changes that seem unbearable at first but are later seen as positive outcomes. Every author's Hero's Journey from chaos to clarity comes to fruition in this next section, *Words of Wisdom and Encouragement: If I Knew Then What I Know Now.*

PART 5

WORDS OF WISDOM AND ENCOURAGEMENT
If I Knew Then What I Know Now

They said she would never bloom.
They were wrong.

Mr. Sandman Bring Me More Dreams for Life
Kathleen O'Keefe-Kanavos

If I knew then what I know now concerning the power of dreams, I would have begun Dream Journaling *before* I needed dream-guidance to save my life. And, I would have advocated much more strongly for my health concerning the medical community and tests on which they relied. If necessary, I would have found new doctors who would listen to me and my health concerns, take me seriously, and act on my behalf concerning necessary medical testing. Mr. Sandman, please bring me more dreams for life.

Dancing Queen
Rev. Patricia Cagganello

If I knew then what I know now, I would have allowed myself the confidence and freedom to more fully express myself—and to dance, and dance, and dance some more.

Always Do the Right Thing
Dennis J. Pitocco

Time and again, throughout our personal and professional lives, we are faced with shortcuts and "the easy way" versus "the right way." Never choose to gain at the expense of someone else losing. Integrity matters. Reputation matters. Always take the high road, even if no one will see you take the low one. Always do the right thing, because you always know the right thing to do. Take that road that is less traveled these days. Because there is no do-over when you take the road most traveled. Be the one who creates a legacy that matters.

All is in Perfect Order
J.S. Drake

I would know that everything I had experienced and will experience is not an accident. In each moment, through the infinite beauty and mastery of my own soul, circumstances and experiences are brought forth for my highest good. Often, my limited perspective did not allow me to see or understand this ingenious design, especially when circumstances brought turmoil. But I know, now, all is in perfect order and perfection *even when it least appears to be so.* So, I choose to apply what I know now and what I'd wish I'd known then: to simply surrender and witness the gifts in all experiences.

234

Knowing Life is Precious
Lynn Forrester

If I had known then what destroying a life within really meant and the impact it would have on me from the ages of eighteen through sixty-nine, I would never have allowed it. Because I lacked confidence, I let someone convince me that the life I carried inside me meant nothing, by using my fear of not having someone to love me. I would have run away from this request, and today I would have a son or daughter who might have been a president, a priest, a father of many children, or even an astronaut. My life would have changed, and the two children God has given me would look at me differently.

Know Thyself
Tamee Knox

If I knew then what I know now, I would have worried less, rejoiced more, and seen the beauty in ALL of creation. My moment-to-moment connection to the Creative Divine would have led me, instead of ego and my belief system. This deep connection allows for self-acceptance and self-love. It is the underlying prerequisite to truth, fulfillment, and Oneness.

Practice Being the Love and the Light
Altair Shyam

If I knew then what I know now about change and transformation, I would have found the time to practice being the love and the light in every moment, more fully, with more presence, and more open to the breath of the universe within me. I would have breathed in the beauty and love of the Divine Mother with every breath. I would have liberated the love breath, up the central astral spine, the *sushumna*, and through the light of the Christ Consciousness at the spiritual eye, with every thought and with total awareness. Breathing in and out, surrendering, letting go. I would have spent more time breathing and practicing stillness, silence, and spacious awareness, sitting in eternal peace.

Trust Your Intuition
Kristi Tornabene

At seventeen, I thought I knew everything about health. Living in the dorm, loving new foods and flavors, I tried them all. Honey, butter, and gravy every night helped me gain the "freshman fifteen." Then, moving to an apartment off-campus and walking to class helped me lose weight and keep it off for twenty years. Weight maintenance seemed simple. Eat better, plan and cook your meals, and walk. I thought I would be a great health coach even then. Then came middle age and a whole new learning experience.

Together We Will Change the World
Peggy Miller

Change that happens through the illness of your child often brings one's life and purpose more fully into examination and question. Reevaluate what is important and what you hope to accomplish, not just in your professional career, but in your life. Slowly begin to make substantial changes in the way you approach life. Specifically, start to pay more attention to your own needs, as well as the needs of others you love.

Bring It On
Anrita Melchizedek

If I knew then what I know now—I wouldn't change a thing. I would still have shouted, "Bring it on, Universe!" My deepest challenges have brought about the greatest Soul blossomings. Surrendering to each moment has forged the ability to see the perceived blessings in all that arises from the heart of compassion and the emptiness of the lower mind. Each step reveals a higher path to love, until love is all there is.

Embrace Change and
Focus on the Silver Lining
Paulette Scales

I have learned to change the way I think. Change now is accepted as a challenge and all doors are tried with the focus on moving forward. Change is an opportunity to alter my perspective from the situation that is presented. Now I look beyond the obstacle for the silver lining, and welcome the new opportunity to recreate, learn, and grow. Change is guiding me on my spiritual path, and I am learning to trust, believe, and act with faith. My strength and courage come from my ability to change!

Self-Awareness for Empowerment
Eileen Bild

I learned through life's trials and tribulations where I was weak, naïve, and disempowered. By increasing awareness of who I am at my core I have become bold, stand in my truths, and teach others how to treat me. Having a strong sense of self and knowing when others are overpowering and/or controlling is empowering. Defined boundaries and being okay to say "No" will strengthen the inner voice, build confidence and increase assertiveness in taking experiences in the direction desired.

Chop Wood, Carry Water
Dr. Jane Galloway

I love this question. It is a kind of Zen Köan, a philosophical puzzle, unsolvable from the perspective of present time. The truth is that if I knew "then" what I know now, NOW would not be now! It would be a reality impacted by what I knew then. Psychic, intuitive and astrological readings have predicted things I now know to be true but that I had to live my way into discovering. Wisdom lies in our next footstep. We know what we know, when we know it.

Mistakes are Miracles
Helen Brennand

Our mistakes are often seen as failure or wrongdoing, leaving us with the feeling of lack or not being good enough. But we miss the magic that is within mistakes. If we can honor and respect mistakes in the same way we do our success, we find fortuitous turning points and markers of growth in our life. Mistakes are the seeds of blossoming miracles. If I had known to embrace every mistake lovingly with an open, forgiving heart, my life journey would have always been one of courage and joy.

And Just Like That! Time Ran Out
Jane Anderson

"Mom, don't use your vacation time for me. I will be home for Thanksgiving in six weeks anyway." My daughter's logic sounded good and I had plans for my 5 days of vacation. I couldn't get her off my mind though, so my husband and I flew to Atlanta for a short Friday to Sunday visit. If I had known then how quickly her life would end, I would have used my entire vacation for her. Those other four vacation days? I don't remember one thing about them. I remember everything about the last one I spent with my daughter. The time we spend with loved ones is non-renewable. There are no do overs. Be careful with your moments because they become your memories.

Note To Self...
Mel Greenberg

If I could pick any age in my youth, and send a note from me today and it would read: Don't worry yourself so about others. Be you! The barrage of opinions, feelings, motivations will come at you, from every angle – LET THEM! You just keep on being you. It will all work out precisely as it is meant to, and you will be happy. Not because your life will be perfect. No, my dear, because it is yours! As you have created it. As you have dreamt it. Now go live it – with love and a smile…

Don't Force - Go with The Flow
Rev. Stephanie Red Feather, PhD

I grew up with very masculine influences, so I learned to force things. I have a strong will and could shove a square peg into a round hole. What I didn't realize was how I had completely overridden my ability to trust, listen, soften, and move through life with ease and flow. I always required the cosmic 2x4 to the forehead because nothing else would break my tunnel vision. If I could go back, I would tell myself, 'There's a reason for the thing not working out. The Universe is trying to point you in another direction. Let go and trust.'

Lesson Learned
Peggy Linsey

If I knew then what I know now about decluttering and downsizing, I would have realized a long time ago that happiness is more about memories than stuff. I would have questioned keeping things I thoughtlessly stashed in a cabinet or in a drawer or on a shelf, simply because there was room for them. I learned that overflowing closets, basements, and attics are a smothering monster. I now know that I would rather have my mind overflow with wonderful memories of time spent with inspirational people at home or in interesting places. Lesson learned.

Shaping the Future
Sara Gouveia

Where are you at this moment of your life? Are you where you'd like to be? Are you still on the path to it, or are you not even near it? I'm sure there are several things you'd like to change if you knew better. But I wouldn't. Despite some regrets I feel. All the lessons were necessary for me to grow and be where I stand right now. I haven't yet reached the peak that I want but I'm working on it. And hopefully, you will too accept your past and do your best today to shape a better future.

From the Old Paradigm to Self-Realization
Glenda-Ray Riviere

If I knew then, what I know now, I would likely not have manifested imbalance in the body and a life-threatening illness. With the awareness that I have now, of integrating lessons behind an experience through Self-realization-- no longer blaming others, allowing All to be completely felt and moved through the body, energy flows and the body returns to balance naturally. In this way, I integrate lessons on the fly, accept my-Self-- all my experiences fully and empower my subconscious to create the life of my heart's desire as the Master Creator of my reality.

Look Inward for Profound, Positive Change
Joan Chadbourne, EdD

When something is missing or just not right with life, look first inside. We're taught to identify the problem's origin as out there so we can change IT. Instead, be willing to ask yourself questions about your hidden thoughts, experiences, fears. Be curious. Be non-judgmental. Be loving. Dig deep. Probe your beliefs. How? Journal, mediate, explore with a listener. Do what works for you until an inner voice tells you, you've identified the core, unconscious belief or experience. You'll be at the root of the situation and be able to weed your garden and plant seeds of meaning and fulfillment.

How My Hope Was Born from Despair
Maria Lehtman

Take heed of your thoughts, sensations in your body, your intuitive wisdom. The essential knowledge in your life does not come from talks and deeds. The sacred intelligence stems from the pauses, breaks in the rhythm, and silence. Tune in to your mind's natural frequencies, and you already know if what you hear and see is the truth, and what the outcome will be. Our life is precious. While we walk alone, we are never left without guidance. Be stubborn to survive the odds, while remaining humble to hear the whispers of quiet wisdom from the Universe.

Fortitude Wins the Battle
Connie Bramer

It's funny how life experiences can change you, even make you stronger. My cancer diagnosis was a fork in the road I was forced to take. It didn't come with a choice of direction or a shortcut to wellness. What I do know is that when I am pulled to the side of adversity, I persevere, and I have learned to make lemonade from lemons and add a splash of vodka.

Life is a Journey, Love is All There Is
Deborah Beauvais

I would wrap myself in love and comfort while journeying through grief and devastation. I would know no one is ever alone as we are guided each and every day. I would know Life on Earth is designed with ebbs and flows with lessons through many experiences. This is the Gift! Yes, we can find inner power through tragedy, but we don't have to continue the struggle by creating thoughts rooted in a victim mindset. We can choose to set ourselves free. Our loved ones want this for us. When we do this, our gratitude grows exponentially, and we find Peace within.

Finding Balance
Denise Alexander Pyle

I would have been less insecure and more confident. Be true to yourself if you want to succeed in life. There are those who work solely to make money and don't care about their clients or customers. Others are power driven, seeking fame or the win at all costs. Just be passionate in what you do and perform to the best of your ability in service to others. You will find balance and your reputation for compassion and justice will provide you all the fame and fortune that you will ever require.

Dare to Voice Your Opinion
Cassandra A. Tindal

If I knew then what I know now, I would have found someone who would listen, and could understand my pain, loneliness, and fears about speaking up.

Expect Miracles
Gina Roda

If I knew then what I know now I would have been more present in my life and embraced self-love and self-value. I know now that things that seem bad somehow turn into good and are often blessings in disguise. Expect miracles.

Known in Loss
Jess Campmans

If I knew then that the deep connection I had to the spirit of the natural world and the animals was actually existential for me to thrive, I would have allowed myself to nurture that connection rather than rejecting it and hiding it deep in fear, in order to fit into the world around me. Knowing now how that deep connection is an essential and existential part of my soul, I would have understood how lost I felt without it.

Lighten Up!
Sora Garrett

I would remind myself to Lighten Up! Most of the changes that define us are going to happen whether or not we embrace them, so we may as well enjoy the journey. My wise-self wants the part of me that gets stressed over the unknown to relax, open her eyes wide in wonder, laugh often, and be grateful for every part of this amazing adventure we call life.

Pay Attention to That Voice
Teresa Velardi

When the priest asked me, "Teresa, do you take this man…" and then I heard the still small voice from deep within my soul say, "Teresa, don't do this," I would have tossed my bouquet, hiked up my dress, and run as fast as I could out of the church to freedom! I've come to recognize the voice of God and have learned to take direction since that day at the marriage altar so long ago. Today, I pay attention to that voice. Taking direction from a Higher Source works out much better than how I would do things.

Believe In Divine Intervention
Ellie Pechet, M.Ed

I would have worried less and trusted more. I would have believed that Divine Intervention was at play as it usually is when events and circumstances go in a direction we didn't anticipate and that everything would end up just the way it was supposed to on a Higher level. If I had known then what I know now, I would have remained in a place of inner peace rather than giving in to stress and worry. The more we trust what comes our way, the smoother the bumps will be as we ride the wave of change.

AFTERWORD

Change to the Rescue
by Kathleen O'Keefe-Kanavos

Without change, I would be dead, and like me,
my stories in the book would be buried.

Change can alter individual lives, create mass evolutions, and transform situations with a simple course correction. Without change, there would be no forward movement of humanity or the world. The metamorphosis can be as small as a seemingly insignificant personal shift in perception or as monumental as a Global-Voice conversion of universal ideas that transition into an evolution, or revolution. Yes, a revolting notion can be a good change hidden beneath fear.

Fear of the unknown is both a change deterrent and catalyst. There is no greater fear than the fear of fear itself, which will herald in change as a means to avoid the unknown. Humans like to feel in control of their destiny. Feeling out-of-control can leave us feeling vulnerable, unstable, and unbalanced.[1] No matter its size or scope, change is a deviation from the norm—our norm—and that can cause stress.

But, without change, I would be dead, and my stories in the book would be buried.

My mother was a registered nurse, so I had been taught from an early age not to challenge the wisdom of any doctors or medical tests. "Whenever a doctor entered a room, we immediately stood and addressed him with respect," my mother said. "We followed his medical orders to the letter, and the doctor's decisions were final and never challenged."

Much has changed since my mother was a young nurse, and I believe the change has been for the better.

The same mammograms, blood tests, and physical exams that failed to detect my breast cancer also failed a second and third time to discover recurrence. The defining moment between my life and death was related to a thought-change taking place on the world stage of health and healing; the rise of the dreaming e-patient.[2] described in my book *Dreams That Can Save Your Life*. Much as dreams are windows into another information highway, the internet was a type of Universal Wisdom Window at my fingertips.

According to Wikipedia[3], the e-patient is an individual or health consumer who participates fully in his or her medical care. This patient is creating a significant change in the medical community and industry for both patients and their doctors.

The desire to live had prompted me to change into a dreaming e-patient. My cancers missed by modern medical tests were found by my recurrent dreams. I imagined I was alone in experiencing dreams that could predict illness, but research showed that guiding dreams have been taking place since the beginning of recorded time, as seen in the Asclepeion Dream Temples[4] of Ancient Egypt, Rome, and Greece. People with challenges slept on the floors of their places of worship, beside their spiritual leaders, to get information from dreams on the changes needed to improve or save their life.

Fast-forward to modern times. Dreams and inner guidance are replaced by modern medicine that focuses on science, not the psyche. But Change stepped in to save the day and my life.

250

To get the medical tests needed to find my cancer and receive treatment, I had to change my view of doctors and testing. It was time to embrace the idea of going back to the future with diagnostic dreams, so rather than blindly accepting test results, I voiced a challenge with the phrase, "Prove me wrong." It was up to me to begin the necessary changes in my life that would trickle into the medical community to embrace healing from the mind to the body, rather than only focusing on the physical with pharmaceuticals.

Saying the word "change" would not suffice. I had to *live* the word.

Convincing my doctors to do exploratory surgery and use a second set of tests to find my cancer caused a domino effect of medical transformation. My perspective on health care, treatment, inner-guidance, and intuition evolved into believing dreams are more than just random firings from a sleeping brain. My medical pathology reports validated the ancient art of Dreaming Healing and became part of a wave of paradigm shifts now flooding the medical community. The idea of combining dreams with modern medicine to achieve healing greater than the sum of its individual parts was a significant course-correction in my own health and wellness. It was change.

Stepping out of my comfort zone as an obedient patient and into my power as a dreaming e-patient was disquieting and new to me, and downright frightening to my family.

I had to practice standing in my power and used Mirror Psychotherapy[5] as a reflective therapeutic practice to help with my inner transition. It is the same technique I used with students in my Special Education classrooms and Psychology 101 class.

Sitting in front of a mirror, I would look myself in the eye and tell me what needed to be changed and why the change was needed. Then "we" discussed how that could best be accomplished. No one knows me better than I know myself, because I've known myself all my life and I've seen everything I've done. When someone told me, "That is a bit schizoid," I stepped into my power and said, "It's time to change that thought. People have been talking to themselves forever, because some of the best answers come from the questions, we dare to ask ourselves." My statement was not said lightly. I lived it.

During my treatment with cancer recurrence, I developed the dreaded white-coat-syndrome, aka Post Traumatic Stress Disorder or PTSD. The sight of anything white made me vomit, including white lines on streets. While curled up in a fetal position in my husband's arms—I made him change out of his white shirt—I remembered something my Green Beret-father had told me during one of my severe cases with a student suffering from PTSD.

"During Vietnam, when soldiers returned home with PTSD, the first step in helping them was getting them to talk—just to talk while someone listened."

In desperation, I sat at the bathroom mirror and tried to look myself in the eyes, but I found it disturbing to face myself. It felt invasive and embarrassing to connect with my inner selves. How silly could I be to allow the color white to make me sick every time I saw it? And how frightening that the color white now held me captive in a bathroom! Two days later, I had talked myself into self-acceptance and out of PTSD. Practicing change set me free.

Learning to embrace transition until it becomes a new habit may take practice. And practice often leads to success by holding two different or even opposing thoughts at the same time: the old method and the new idea of change. We must consider and weigh the benefits of the diversity involved.

The act of being aware of differing viewpoints is the first step in adaptation to change.

Author F. Scott Fitzgerald explained this concept beautifully when he said, "The test of a first-rate intelligence is the ability to hold two opposed ideas in mind at the same time and still retain the ability to function."[6]

Although we may inherently avoid change, the transition has many psychological and emotional benefits. Case in point: Who wants to live in dirty diapers forever? Time for a change!

As many of the true stories in the book point out, even change resulting from the heartbreak of losing someone you consider the love of your life, or a beloved pet like the turtle Ellie Jr., can be a growth catalyst[7] by helping us advance personally, emotionally and psychologically. It forces us to mentally view life in a manner that is different from that to which we have become accustomed, and it may be in complete opposition to our current beliefs and systems.

We must step out of our comfort zone and think "outside the box" of social acceptability.

The shift in perception may challenge existing values and beliefs and the systems and platforms on which they have been built, including family, peers, traditions, and education, as seen in Eileen Bild's true story, *Shift Your Focus for Change.*

Without the ability to adapt to change, a creature, culture, or species will cease to exist. Change is part of the advancement of life. The inability to adapt to change is extinction. Survival of the fittest is really about the survival of the mentally and emotionally strong enough to embrace transformation.

The fossils of Tyrannosaurus rex and the 1,100-pound Saber-toothed tiger[8] attest to this fact. Although these were considered the most physically fit and strongest of the ancient dinosaurs and mammals, it was smart humans who physically and psychologically adapted to the changes taking place on the planet. Their decisions allowed a species living in rock-caves to evolve into modern people living in smart-homes.

Change can reveal your strengths and define limitations that can result in new psychological boundaries that can work.

Flexibility is the key to successful change, exemplified in Paulette Scales' story, *Try All Doors*. Think of change as something that gets you out of your rut. By embracing change and meeting it head-on with excitement, you can learn not to be set in your ways and to maintain a more positive attitude. Flexibility can allow you to become more compassionate and less judgmental by giving you the opportunity to discover new cultures and ways of thinking about other people, and what it is like to "walk a mile in their shoes." It reminds you to be kind when considering the choices other people may make.

Alternately, change may reinforce your trust in the belief system you already have. Either way, you become stronger. It is often when we are most challenged that new opportunities present themselves in the form of change.

By discovering new ways to approach problems, you may learn something new about you.

Routines can become a rut and contribute to depression and stress. A change in routine keeps your mind active by refocusing your thoughts onto positive thought patterns.

When presented with an intimidating change, remind yourself of all the positive impacts that shift could create, not only in your own life but in the lives of those around you as well.

But what would be the positive aspects of choosing the path of change when feeling lost like a babe in the woods of life? The answer may be best explained in the poem *The Road Not Taken* by Robert Frost.

> *I shall be telling this with a sigh*
> *Somewhere ages and ages hence:*
> *Two roads diverged in a wood, and I—*
> *I took the one less traveled by,*
> *And that has made all the difference.*[9]

So, the next time you hear yourself say, "I need a change!" embrace it. Flap your butterfly wings and know they are felt in some manner throughout Universal Oneness. Dare to take a new path. Don't just mean the words. *Live* the words, because change is good.

What's the Plan, Stan?

by Rev. Patricia Cagganello

Change is our golden nugget.

It has been an honor to co-create this book with brilliant souls from around the globe. As our stories of change have been shared and read, we and our world are forever changed.

Our lives are not always easy. Like many of you, my life has changed dramatically over the past several years. I have cried an ocean of tears and my belief in myself has been sorely tested. Truth be told, on multiple occasions, I have been known to raise my fist and shake it at the Universe, objecting to my perceived unfairness of it all.

Change in our lives is constant, and it can be a great catalyst for personal and spiritual growth. However, sometimes we can impede our growth or cause more stress in our lives, not because of the change, but because of our perception of the change. I offer this lighthearted story I wrote a few years ago as an illustration.

What's the plan, Stan?

"What's the plan, Stan?" is such a great saying. My dad used to say it to me, and I find myself saying it to my kids. "What's the plan, Stan?" I ask lightheartedly when they are getting ready to go out with friends or when we are planning our day. "What's the plan, Stan?" I'll text to check in with them and see what is going on.

It's a simple, almost whimsical question. It brings a sense of levity to a situation, making it seem less overbearing. There is something about rhyming that makes even a difficult query seem a little easier.

So, I thought I would try it out on a bigger question, a question I have had since my divorce a few years ago. It's a question that I have kept tucked in the far recesses of my brain since I decided to quit my job and follow my spiritual path—a question that, as time goes on and I don't see major life and career changes happening quickly enough, peeks its head out more and more, trying to get my attention.

I take a deep breath as my heart is racing. Bringing my question forth and exposing it to the light of day will make it very real. I won't be able to tuck it neatly back into my brain and pretend it isn't there. I will have to deal with it. I'm not sure I'm ready, but I know I also can't ignore it any longer. So here it goes…

"What am I going to do with the rest of my life, and how am I going to support myself?" I finally give an anxious voice to the question that has troubled me for so long.

Whoa! Well that was overwhelming, to say the least. Putting "the rest of my life" and "support myself" in the same question was probably not a great idea. Either question on its own is a lot to handle and would make even the strongest of people feel a little weak in the knees.

But wait a minute. Why is it a lot to handle? Is it because of the words I used? The way I phrased it? Is it because of the way I am making the question so all-encompassing, or possibly because it is charged with my anxiety and my fear? Is it the knowledge that the last remnants of my old identity, the me I have known for so long and feel comfortable with, has to change?

Wow, that's the golden nugget I was looking for: change.

That's it, really. The underlying emotion we feel in almost every situation has to do with how we are perceiving change. If we perceive change as something to be feared or something to be lost, then it creates a sense of anxiety.

As I reread my words above— "the last remnants of my old identity, the me I have known for so long…"—I see they are riddled with a sense of fear and loss. My whole thought process surrounding the imminent change that is upon me is that I am going to be worse off than I am now. I will be losing a part of myself, my identity.

Whether the change happens because a relationship ends, our children grow up and leave home, or our careers are changing or ending, it doesn't matter. Whether the change is our choice usually doesn't matter, either. We still feel a sense of loss and a sense of fear of the unknown that somehow the future won't be as good as what we know now.

But what if we think of it, this change that is upon us, in a different way?

What if we embrace change as an inevitable and wondrous part of life? What if we are grateful for an opportunity to grow and evolve, and we immerse ourselves in a process of self-discovery? What if we know in our hearts that, as we grow, we expand our body of life experiences, not diminish them or us in any way?

Maybe the key to handling life and the inevitable changes we will experience is really all in our perception. Possibly, it's even more simply in the delivery of the questions.

So, I'll try it a different way.

"What's the plan, Stan?" I ask myself with a smile.

Enjoy your journey.

Thank you for joining us as we traveled together through the heart of our shared humanity. May your life be blessed with experiences of great change and may you be a blessing to others.

Much love,
Patricia

ADDITIONAL READING

A Book of Miracles: Inspiring True Stories of Healing, Gratitude, and Love– October 21, 2014, New World Library, Dr. Bernie S. Siegel (Author)

Love, Animals, and Miracles: Inspiring True Stories Celebrating the Healing Bond – October 27, 2015, New World Library, Dr. Bernie S. Siegel (Author)

Dreams That Can Save Your Life: Early Warning Signs of Cancer and Other Diseases – April 17, 2018; Findhorn/Inner Traditions, Larry Burk M.D. C.E.H.P. (Author), Kathleen O'Keefe-Kanavos (Author), Bernie Siegel M.D. (Foreword)

Surviving Cancerland: Intuitive Aspects of Healing – March 28, 2014 Cypress House, Kathleen O'Keefe-Kanavos (Author)

God is in the Little Things: Messages from the Animals – republished June 26, 2016; Sacred Stories Publishing, Patricia Brooks (Author)

God is in the Little Things: Messages from the Golden Angels –republished May 30, 2016; Sacred Stories Publishing, Patricia Brooks (Author)

Scanning For Signal – November 17, 2016; Sacred Stories Publishing, Patricia Brooks (Co-Author)

The Power of 1(0): A Guide to Living the Ten Commandments and the Golden Rule in Modern Times – February 22, 2018, Balboa Press, Denise Alexander Pyle (Author)

How Connie Got Her Rack Back: A Breast Cancer Memoir – February 2, 2018, Friesen Press, Constance Bramer (Author)

The Gateways: The Wisdom of 12-Step Spirituality – September 27, 2016, Sacred Stories Publishing, Jane Galloway (Author)

Children's Garden: Blessed Mother's Holy Spring of Youthful Hearts Kindle Edition, May 25, 2011, eAuthorHouse, Lynn Forrester (Author)

Running With Our Eyes Closed – October 16, 2018, 4 Pillars Publishing, Mel Greenberg (Author)

May I Only Leave Rose Petals – April 9, 2019, Garnet Press, J.S. Drake (Author)

Transformative Meditation: A Guide of Multidimensional Healing Journeys to Transform and Empower All Aspects of Your Life – July 26, 2018, Balboa Press, Glenda-Ray Riviere (Author)

Belief – May 2014, Creative Locations, Ltd., Helen Brennand (Author)

The Evolutionary Empath: A Practical Guide for Heart-Centered Consciousness, November 5, 2019, Inner Traditions, Rev. Stephanie Red Feather, PhD (Author)

Healing Conversations Now, February 26, 2011, The Taos Institute, Joan Chadbourne (Co-Author)

Pebbles in the Pond: Transforming the World One Person at a Time, Wave Four, June 9, 2015, Transformation Books, Tamee Knox (Contributing Author)

Conversations That Make a Difference: Shift Your Beliefs to Get What You Want, June 29, 2014, Teresa Velardi (Contributing Author)

Ignite Your Inner Star, Dec 2, 2016, Shine Publishing, Sora Garrett (Co-Author)

The Miracle Keys, Nov 11, 2014, Shine Publishing, Sora Garrett (Author)

Silent Grace, July 11, 2011, Inspired Connections, Sora Garrett (Author)

Intuition at Work: Pathways to Unlimited Possibilities, September 1, 1998, New Leaders Press, Sora Garrett (Contributing Author)

Hitching A Ride: A Guide to Earthbound Spirits and How They Affect You, October 1, 2015, CreateSpace, Ellie Pechet M.Ed. (Author)

Diary of a Yogi: A Book of Awakening, September 20, 2018, Balboa Press, Guan Shi Yin (Author)

BOOK CLUB QUESTIONS

1. What story of change in the book impacted you the most and why?
2. What advice would you give to the author of the story in question #1?
3. Why do you think change is important for the progress of the human race?
4. Are you surprised that people from across the globe experienced similar change events and emotions? Why or why not?
5. Do you believe that spiritual transformation can occur due to a significant change in one's life? Why or why not?
6. Which story in the book exemplified the most profound change, and which one exemplified the least amount of change?

CONTRIBUTING AUTHORS

Dr. Bernie Siegel is an American writer and retired pediatric surgeon who writes on the relationship between the patient and the healing process. He is known for his New York Times best-seller *Peace, Love and Healing.* Bernie has been named one of the top twenty Spiritually Influential Living People on the Planet by the Watkins Review and he was also named a 2018 V.I.P. Spiritual Leaders Top Pick for his work and lifetime achievements. berniesiegelmd.com

Jane Anderson has professional experience scattered across industries from financial services to engineering and manufacturing. Her background in writing and editing website content is the foundation of her current love of social media. Jane is a columnist for BIZCATALYST 360°

Deborah Beauvais, founder/owner of syndicated Dreamvisions 7 Radio Network, hosts her own show, Love By Intuition, as well as Empowered Connections. Deborah is a mentor, the founder of Kids 4 Love Project and Kids 4 Love Project Radio Show, which celebrates kids who make a difference. She's a Reconnective Healing™ and The Reconnection™ Practitioner. Deborah is publishing her first children's book, *The Paper Doll Kids*, co-written with Janine Ouelette Sullivan. dreamvisions7radio. com

Eileen Bild is CEO of Ordinary to Extraordinary Life, Core Thinking. She holds a Masters degree in Transpersonal Psychology, is a Certified Life Coach, LMT, Executive Producer for OTEL Productions, and a columnist for BIZCATALYST 360°. eileenbild.com

Connie Bramer, Founder and President of Get Your Rack Back Inc., is a published author of *How Connie Got Her Rack Back* and an accomplished speaker on topics related to surviving breast cancer, overcoming adversity, and women's empowerment. gyrb.org

Helen Brennand, author of the book *Belief*, is an equine professional based in England, an accomplished rider, trainer, and holistic therapist. She has a passion for horse welfare and respects them as sentient beings. Complementing her writing, Helen's time is now dedicated to her horse sanctuary, The Haven, founded to ensure a lasting and safe place where a horse's inner wisdom is free to be released and allowed to shine. belief444.com

Jess Campmans is a shamanic energy intuitive who guides soul-purpose empowerment, enabling intrinsic authentic communication and connection and claiming of our sacred heritage through the universal wisdom of the horse. jesscampmans.com

Joan Chadbourne, EdD is an author, coach, facilitator, and speaker who lives what she writes. Joan has a doctorate in Counseling Psychology from UMass. She has co-authored the book *Healing Conversations Now* and published articles on relationships, positive aging, strength-based change, and intuition. joanchad.com and healingconversationsnow.com

J.S. Drake is an author and poet. Her book of poetry *May I Only Leave Rose Petals* helps others find their light in the face of darkness. thisroaditravel.com

Rev. Stephanie Red Feather, Ph.D. is the author of the book *The Evolutionary Empath: A Practical Guide for Heart-Centered Consciousness.* As an ordained shamanic minister, her passion is to help fellow empaths embrace their soul's calling to evolve humanity to the next stage of consciousness. www.bluestartemple.org

Lynn Forrester is an author and retired police officer, a former member of the Olympic Shooting Team, and the first female member of the elite SWAT team. She is a columnist for BIZCATALYST 360° and has published a children's book titled, *Children's Garden.* Lynn is a devout Catholic who resides in Houston TX.

Dr. Jane S. Galloway is the author of *The Gateways: The Wisdom of 12-Step Spirituality / Dynamic Practices That Work* and founder of T.R.I.B.E. Transformation /Realization /Inspiration /Belonging /Expression. Dr. Galloway is also a career actor, ordained minister, painter, and playwright. janegalloway.com

Sora Garrett is a life-simplification guide and philanthropreneur who helps people move from overwhelm to overflow with her writing, mentoring, and collaborative giving programs. Find her books, courses, and free inspiration at soragarrett.com

Sara Gouveia practices equine medicine in the United Kingdom and offers personal and professional coaching techniques to help the veterinary community. petsolving.com

Mel Greenberg is a mom, wife, writer, and survivor. Mel is also the author of *Running With Our Eyes Closed*. "I've 'survived' more than some, less than many: adolescence, losing my mom to breast cancer during those years, college, dating, marriage, childbirth, youth sports, turning forty, breast cancer, turning fifty. And more than all of it, I've survived the empty nest." melmediallc.com

Tamee Knox is a contributing author to the #1 international best-selling book series *Pebbles in the Pond: Transforming the World One Person at a Time, Wave Four*. She is dedicated to using multiple dimensions, the energy field, breath, sound, and sacred geometry to complement healing, balance, and wisdom. shekhinahpath.com

Maria Lehtman has more than twenty years of experience in the telecommunications and travel industry. She currently works in International Sales & Marketing. Maria specializes in digital photography and writing about digital and self-transformation. She is a columnist for BIZCATALYST 360°

Peggy Linsey is the author of *This New Cottage*, a tale of color, nostalgia, and the challenges of rebuilding a Cape Cod cottage. The coffee-table book features her personal story and photographs of the cottage rebuild. thisnewcottage.com

Peggy Miller heads The Male Breast Cancer Coalition (MBCC), a non-profit patient advocacy organization which brings everyone together to educate the world about male breast cancer. malebreastcancercoalition.org

Anrita Melchizedek was born with many of her ESP gifts already activated and in communication with the Company of Heaven. As a Soul Reader, Master Healer, and Light Weaver, Anrita sees the Light codes of potentiality within energy fields and draws from these Light codes and blueprints when assisting in the healings of others. voicesofthelighttribe.com and pleiadianlight.net

Ellie Pechet, M.Ed. is an author and highly trained metaphysician with thirty-four years of professional counseling and healing experience. In her private practice as an intuitive counselor, medium, shaman and metaphysician, Ellie helps clients from all over the world by using her proven Distance Healing, Intuitive Therapy, and the Pechet Healing Technique. phoenixrisinghealing.com

Dennis Pitocco is founder, publisher, and Editor-in-Chief of BIZCATALYST 360°, the award-winning business, culture, and lifestyle multimedia digest, serving as the global hub for enhanced performance and well-being. Read more about it here – @BC360° He is also founder and Chief Encouragement Officer of GoodWorks 360°, a virtual non-profit social enterprise dedicated to providing mission-critical, *pro bono* services to good nonprofits worldwide.

Denise Alexander Pyle, an attorney and expert in family law for more than forty-three years, received her law degree from Michigan State University School of Law. She authored *The Power of 1(0), a Guide to Living the Ten Commandments in Modern Times* and has published various professional articles as well as opinion pieces. denisealexanderpyle.com and dapylelaw.com

Glenda-Ray Riviere is an Energy Healer Intuitive and author of the book *Transformative Meditation*. Offering personal and group sessions, Glenda holds sacred space in the transformation and empowerment of others, journeying them back to their heart to integrate healing through Self-realization. reikiandbeyond-glendaray.com

Gina Roda has an extraordinary ability to understand relationship dynamics and is able to easily identify positive solutions. With clarity, compassion, joy, and humor, she provides a positive, life-supporting environment that fosters personal evolution. She builds bridges of understanding, cooperation, and unity and therefore, is able to effectively mediate peaceful resolutions. theartofconsciouscoaching.com

Paulette Scales worked in mental health for thirty-seven years. After retirement, she embarked on a spiritual journey looking for something her soul lacked. She was raised with a strict religious background, but didn't find it satisfying, despite her connection with God. "The changes in my life that transpired over this past year are astonishing. Changing my emotions changes my life story!" trydoors.com

Altair Shyam is a teacher, healer, and mystic who guides the way of love, unity, and harmony for the New Gaia. He has an extensive background in healing, teaching, and education and holds degrees and certifications in counseling and alternative health, business, and mindful education. He has written nine books including a best-seller, a children's book series, and a spiritual biography. altairshyam.com

Cassandra A. Tindal is a co-author, writer, professional life coach, and the visionary founder and Executive Producer of Womenz Straight Talk Television, including Editor-in-Chief of Womenz Straight Talk Magazine, a publication that focuses on real stories that matter, to enlighten, empower, and raise the social consciousness and awareness of a global society. womenzstraighttalktv.net

Kristi Tornabene, author of *Keys to Basic Health-Proactive Strategies for Healthy Aging,* has always been interested in health and well-being. Kristi says, "Without your health, nothing else is possible." keystobasichealth. com

Teresa Velardi is an author, speaker, publisher, and potter. Committed to making a difference in the lives of others, she uses her gifts to help people get their stories told in books. teresavelardi.com

ABOUT THE AUTHORS

Rev. Patricia Cagganello is CEO and Founder of Sacred Stories Media, a conscious online media network. Sacred Stories Media includes Sacred Stories Publishing, an award-winning traditional book publishing and marketing company; Garnet Press a self-publishing book division; and Sacred U, an online course division.

As an ordained interfaith, interspiritual minister Patricia believes every story is a sacred story. She is ordained from One Spirit Interfaith Seminary in New York and has earned her Masters of Arts in Education and her Bachelors of Science in Business. Patricia worked in the corporate and educational worlds for many years and proudly served six years as a sergeant in the U.S. Marine Corps.

Patricia is the author of two books sharing the beginning of her spiritual journey— *God is in the Little Things: Messages from the Animals* and *God is in the Little Things: Messages from the Golden Angels*—and is co-author of a poetry book, *Scanning For Signal.*

Learn more at sacredstoriesmedia.com and sacredstoriespublishing.com

Kathleen (Kat) O'Keefe-Kanavos is accredited in Psychopathology and Special Education. Kat taught Psychology at USF, Ft. Myers Branch, and taught the severely emotionally handicapped for ten years and was Special Education Department Head for two years before retiring.

Kat is also known as The Queen of Dreams in her syndicated columns and PR Guru, video podcaster/radio show host *Dreaming Healing*. A three-time breast cancer survivor whose dreams diagnosed her illness missed by the medical community and the tests on which they relied, she is also a multi-award-winning author and Dream Expert who has been seen on Dr. Oz, Doctors, NBC, and CBS. Kat and Duke University Radiologist Dr. Larry Burk co-wrote the 2018 Nautilus Award Winner, *Dreams That Can Save Your Life*.

She's an international author/lecturer and keynote speaker who promotes patient advocacy and connecting with Divine-guidance through Dreams for success in health, wealth, and relationships. "Don't tell God how big your problems are. Tell your problems how big your God is."

Learn more at kathleenokeefekanavos.com

ENDNOTES

Foreword

1. https://www.goodreads.com/quotes/31183-what-the-caterpillar-calls-the-end-of-the

2. Man's Search for Meaning by Viktor Frankl https://www.goodreads.com/book/show/4069.Man_s_Search_for_Meaning

Psychology of Change

1. https://pure.roehampton.ac.uk/portal/en/persons/leigh-gibson(931e3e80-77b0-4f32-8f04-92e98cc424dd).html/

2. *Dreams That Can Save Your Life: Early Warning Signs of Cancer and Other Diseases;* Findhorn, April 17, 2018, by Burk M.D. C.E.H.P., Larry (Author), Kathleen O'Keefe-Kanavos (Author), Siegel M.D., Bernie (Foreword)

Dreaming, Healing Again! by Kathleen O'Keefe-Kanavos

1. Excerpts taken from *Surviving Cancerland: Intuitive Aspects of Healing;* Kathleen O'Keefe-Kanavos, Cypress House (2014), chapter 3, pg 18

2. Excerpts taken from *Surviving Cancerland: Intuitive Aspects of Healing;* Kathleen O'Keefe-Kanavos, Cypress House (2014) chapter 42 and 43 pages 252- 260

Part 1 Final Thoughts

1. http://steve-patterson.com/love-insanity-austrian-economics/
2. http://www.mbetancourt.com/her/
3. https://www.history.com/topics/india/taj-mahal
4. https://www.psychologytoday.com/us/blog/emotional-fitness/201101/the-ten-most-important-things-remember

Part 2 Final Thoughts

1. https://www.healthline.com/nutrition/happiness-and-health

Part 3 Final Thoughts

1. Shear MK. Complicated grief treatment: the theory, practice, and outcomes. Bereave Care.2010;29:10–14. [PMC free article] [PubMed] [Google Scholar]
2. https://www.ncbi.nlm.nih.gov/pmc/articles/PMC3384444/

Part 4 Final Thoughts

1. https://www.keepbelieving.com/sermon/the-most-sought-after-things-in-the-world/
2. https://www.mayoclinic.org/healthy-lifestyle/stress-management/in-depth/positive-thinking/art-20043950

Afterword

1. https://ideas.repec.org/b/oxp/obooks/9780195118711.html
2. *Dreams That Can Save Your Life: Early Warning Signs of Cancer and Other Diseases*; ch 4; pg 41-43
3. https://en.wikipedia.org/wiki/E-patient
4. https://en.wikipedia.org/wiki/Asclepeion
5. https://scholar.google.com/scholar?q=mirror+therapy+psychotherapy&hl=en&as_sdt=0&as_vis=1&oi=scholart
6. https://www.brainyquote.com/quotes/f_scott_fitzgerald_100572

7. https://www.attitudeisaltitude.com/blog/7-reasons-embracing-change-can-be-a-good-thing/

8. https://www.thoughtco.com/facts-about-the-saber-tooth-tiger-1093337

9. https://www.poetryfoundation.org/poems/44272/the-road-not-taken

Made in the USA
Columbia, SC
17 February 2020